CLOVER, A LITERARY RAG, VOL. 4

CLOVER A LITERARY RAG, VOLUME 4   WINTER, 2012

EDITOR-IN-CHIEF: MARY ELIZABETH GILLILAN
CO-EDITOR: NORMAN L. GREEN
COVER DESIGN: BECCA SHEW

PUBLISHED BY: THE INDEPENDENT WRITERS' STUDIO

203 W. HOLLY SUITE 306

BELLINGHAM, WA 98225

360-961-4477

www.independentwritersstudio.com

ALL RIGHTS RESERVED

© 2012 ALL RIGHTS RESERVED   ISBN 978-0-9644683-4-4

PRINTED BY: THRESHOLD DOCUMENTS

810 NORTH STATE STREET

BELLINGHAM, WA 98225

360-647-7565

The Independent Writers' Studio thanks Stephanie Cosky Hopkinson for her proofreading assistance. Cheers to IWS members for patience & support. Special thanks to David Lee & Robert Hodgson VanWagoner for IWS workshops & to Samuel Green & Dave for letting their friends know about *Clover*. Norman L. Green — you continue to be the best. meg iws

CLOVER
A LITERARY RAG

VOLUME 4 .... WINTER 2012

CONTENTS CONTINUED

Straw Into Gold	Petersen	71-72
Sutra and Syntax	Erickson	73
Walk to the Ride	duMaurier	74
December Snow	Kendall	75
No Marrow	Laws	76-77
Haiku	Shattuck McBride	78
...Dream of Love	Carter	79-80
Unlimited Absolutes	Reese	81-82
First Walks	Oakley	83-84
Choice	Bertolino	85
At Adrianne's	Powell	86
Wine Dark Sea	Samuel Green	87
Sometimes	Azrael	88
Book Review	Daley	89
Lovebugs, Part Two	Patterson	90
Guitar	Takacs	91-92
The Wedding	Woods	93-101
Lethe's Poppy	Petersen	102
Guilty	Takacs	103-104
Four Questions And	Wahtola Trommer	105-106
...Shadow...of the Wasatch	Vause	107-108
Ancestor	Shumaker	109
The Pass Over	Powell	110
Girl, Gathering	Rust	111
Gooseberry	Samuel Green	112
Daylight	Simard	113
Sumas Mt. Meditation	Bertolino	114

CLOVER
A LITERARY RAG

VOLUME 4 .... WINTER 2012

CONTENTS CONTINUED

The Royal Hudson	Kendall	115
A New Sound	Ostler	116-117
Tree Reflections	Scott	118
Bellingham Coal Train	Frost	119-120
Two Views ... Wreckage	Morgan	121
Arrival	Allen	122
Greenways	Cosky Hopkinson	123
Scar	Jon D. Lee	124-140
Art Appreciation	Carter	141
Troubled Colloquy	Bertolino	142
Feels So Good	Reese	143
Can You See Her Fly	Canyon	144
The Wall	Perchik	145
Origins of Geography	Pahmeier	146-147
Delivery	Gillilan	148-149
Giving Voice	Boyle	150-151
My Grandma Nelle	Kendall	152
Evening	Azrael	153
Checking the Boat	Samuel Green	154-155
From a Journal	Morgan	156-157
Quelcid	Harris	158-159
How the Motmot	Shumaker	160
And Still	Azrael	161
I Don't Remember	Canyon	162
Baja Healing	Ostler	163-164
...The Change	Sally Green	165-167
Wheatridge	Phillis	168

CLOVER
A LITERARY RAG

Volume 4 .... Winter 2012

CONTENTS CONTINUED

Tanka	Shattuck McBride	169
Dad, Belly Up	Clarke	170
Driving Dad	Pahmeier	171-172
Spring Burial	Harrison	173
Ghosts	Reeves	174-197
Santa Cruz Boardwalk	Cosky Hopkinson	198-199
Daffodils, This Time	Samuel Green	200
On The Loss	Jon D. Lee	201
When Light	Ostler	202
The Chords	O'Daly	203-204
The Apartment, Later	Morgan	205
December Visit	Kendall	206
Thus the World	Bullis	207
A Step Too Far	Hunter	208
...Scream at a Pony	Curtis	209
Beyond Her Lost Self	Hunter	210
The Handout	O'Daly	211
Barbara	Faulkner	212-218
Blame	Crist	219-221

Editors Note: We deeply regret the technical error made upon the publication of Ms. Pahmeier's poem, Aunt Mabel and the Legless Veteran, *in* Clover, A Literary Rag, Vol. 3. *Ms. Pahmeier is the author of* The House on Breakaheart Road *and also the author of three chapbooks, the most recent of which,* Shake It and It Snows, *won the 2009 Coal Hill Chapbook Award from Autumn House Press. In 2007, she received the Governor's Award for Excellence in the Arts from the state of Nevada. Here is the poem in full:*

Aunt Mabel and the Legless Veteran

Gailmarie Pahmeier

Robert knows he's lucky to be an assistant
professor in a small college town in a southern
state where everyone loves his school,
has a regional tolerance for many
oddities associated with academics,
but his arrest for drunken driving
still stings, picture in the paper, a bad
one, the suspended license rendering
him back to biking the town like a grad
student, and now he's to choose
his community service: 20 hours folding clothes
at Goodwill or a weekend with Herb,
a nearly blind senior citizen
known to tire most caretakers within minutes
with long walks and longer stories.
Robert chooses Herb, tells his young and very
pregnant wife, how bad could it be?

On Saturday, there are many stops
for groceries, prescriptions, cigarettes.
Herb buys one pack of Camels each month,
says even the ridiculous sin tax
can't stop him, he's like anyone's old
Aunt Mabel, he lives alone and needs some

Pahmeier, con't.

pleasure, and if that comes to him by striking
a match and taking a long drag, those bastards
have no compassion, who do they think fought
the commies, and how do they think men became
friends? Sharing smokes, that's how. So the voters
are actually against friendship, see, and against
allowing a lonely old woman some
pleasure as she leans out her window, sits
on her own porch. Herb says his baby daughter
was a smoker, and imagining Herb
as a young father, Robert thinks this woman
must be in her fifties now, full of flesh,
how hard it must be to see your own daughter
as middle aged, how hard to know she's probably
desired by no man, and then Herb says she's dead,
her brain exploded, when they cut her open
and divvied up her parts, her lungs were good,
went, Herb's sure, to a lesser human.

On Sunday there are no necessary
errands, so Herb wants to walk all day,
mosey down to the railroad tracks, watch
for a BNSF engine, not common,
but most certainly beautiful, Herb and his
wife rode the Super Chief on their honeymoon,
went west to see Indians, he bought her
a blossom necklace, they ate on real china
in the dining car, there were most certainly
movie stars on board, his wife wore white gloves.
His daughter, Herb says, once rode the Amtrak
from Seattle to Chicago just to meet
him for a Cubs game, she was that good a girl.
Outside the stadium sat a legless
man with a sign—Vet Needs Help—and they gave
him ten dollars, it was so obvious
the man wasn't faking it, had really
no legs, so, Herb says, a fin each seemed OK,
but you can't trust everyone with a sign,
some of them are just lazy, some fools,

Pahmeier, con't.

some bona fide drug addicts. But a legless
old man, vet or not, sure could use a cold one
and dog, right? Right, Mr. Smarty Pants?

On his way home to his lovely wife,
Robert stops to buy her a carton
of lemonade, her craving today.
He leans his bike against the newspaper stand,
imagines who will walk next with Herb,
how riding a bike around town isn't
really all that bad, but maybe if he took
up walking he'd have more time to think
and maybe he'd think of a name for his
unborn daughter and maybe it will be
an old-fashioned name like Edna or Thelma
or Ethel or Miriam or Mabel.
That's it. Maybelle. That's what he'll tell his wife
tonight as she drinks lemonade, he gin.

Monroe

David Lee

Monroe Newberry's life turned on a pivot
the first day of class his fifth grade year
when he met Mr. Byron Edgers
the first male elementary school teacher
in the history of our town
who in order to get to know his class
began the day calling roll backwards
to let them know his class was going to be different
which resulted in him calling Troy Newberry before Monroe
asked him all the appropriate questions
then Monroe next and said
Are yall you and Troy twin brothers then?

Monroe said No
which was about the length of most sentences he spoke
Troy he's almost two years oldern Monroe is, said Butch Bowen
I asked Monroe, not you said Mr. Byron Edgers
let him speak for hisself
how come you're in the same fifth grade class?
Monroe didn't say anything
looked across the room at Troy
who was busy staring out the window
I asked you a question Monroe Newberry
now you have to answer it said Mr. Byron Edgers
Monroe only scrunched his shoulders
Monroe Newberry I axed you a question
he said turning red in the face

Because I failt fifth grade said Troy Newberry
I have to do it over again
which would have been fine except
the whole fifth grade class excepting Monroe
laughed

That's all right hollered Troy
least I'm not a dummy and I've got a man's name Troy

David Lee, con't.

not some movie star womern's name Monroe
Shut up Troy said Monroe
Oh tell everbody how Mama
wanted you to be her purdy little girl
grow up to be all beautiful in the picture shows
had the name Marilyn Monroe Newberry picked out for you
how she'd say You're my purdy little boy
purdy enough to be my purdy girl Marilyn Monroe
Shut up Troy said Monroe
How she brought you a yellar dress
for your third birthday put it on you

Monroe Newberry jumped up
ran over and pulled his brother Troy out of his chair
on the floor his arms swinging like a tilterwhirl
screaming Shut up Shut up
before Mr. Byron Edgers could pull him away
Troy had a bloody nose and a piece of his ear bitten off
then at recess hit him on the side of the head
with Janette Hutto's roller skate
they had to take him to the school Nurse

Mr. Byron Edgers transferred Monroe Newberry
To Gordon Hamilton's wife
Mrs. Johnnie Hamilton's fifth grade section
for the good of the school
Principal Ellis Mills called the daddy
D'Wayne Newberry in to settle it down
Mrs. Newberry already gone
some said dead some said
living with kin in Arkansas some
said in an insane asylum
he said he didn't know what to do
with them boys they was always
at one another one way or the othern
this was the first time he known
Monroe to get the best of old Troy

for the next two years
no one heard a sound from Monroe Newberry's lips
his teachers said he was tongue tied

David Lee, con't.

school Nurse said he was born defected
Principal Mills who was a church Deacon said
It might be the Lord's touch
students and friends knew Monroe was in there
he just wasn't riding the escalator

until the day in seventh grade
when he discovered Hooter Hagin's genuine birth defect
said out loud Jesust Hooter
you only got one tiddy
and the little Dutch boy named Jan
took his finger out of the dike

language began to trickle syllables then words first
few sentences longer than three words
then five
bursts of sudden shyness and reversion
disorientation and confusion
slowly he rejoined us
word by word by sentence by month by day
and then the Saturday
Troy Newberry and his chosen friends and disciples
captured Monroe in his bedroom
told him they were going to find out
if Marilyn Monroe Newberry had a pecker or not
and then maybe cut it off
to see if he'd holler about that at least

screams so loud calls went to the station
and the fire alarm sounded
Deputy Sheriff Junior Shepherd from one side of town
Sheriff Red Floyd from the other
raced the fire truck to the Newberry residence

found four pubescent
hoodlum-in-training eighth grade boys bloody
bruised and battered
scratch and teeth marks asunder
like red silk ribbons flowing in abundance
mauled and abandoned wailing aftermath hog hounds
Troy Newberry nowhere to be found

David Lee, con't.

Monroe in the front yard
holding a broken bed slat in one hand
a ball peen hammer in the other
crowing like a bantum rooster

for the good of the School Board
Troy Newberry was allowed to
drop out of junior high school early
and at the same time take Driver's Training
to get his license on his fourteenth birthday
moved in with his uncle Cephas Bilberry
and took up immediately with his obese Scotch-eyed daughter
Monroe finished the year
graduated from junior high the next

then went off radar
disappearing into the realm of myth and legend
for seven years until someone saw the advertisement
in the Dispatch and elevated it to first page rumor mill status
Notice to all Men 17 or older:
You are invited by your Uncle Sam
to come to the U S Army Recruitment Office
3006 24th Street Lubbock, Texas
see Staff Sergeant Monroe Newberry
to inquire regarding Career Opportunity
under the Guaranteed Europe Enlistment Policy

and even Mr. Byron Edgers
who was by then the Grade School Principal said
at the monthly Board meeting
Well maybe there is a God after all
and a happy ending besides in fairy tales
but who'd a thunk it?
Johnny Bert Ezell
Head of the School Board that night
whispered Good boy
I knew you could do it

Tomorrow

Michael Daley

I've forgotten how to grip my fat black pen.
It slips around, spongy in my fingers.
A pen born to leak genius, it forgets
glyphs I shaped from an ink well
in mean Mrs. Nealy's dim first grade.
Palmer method embalmed—
drowned in my curlicues like river eddies—
my palm's map hides hills, embankments,
fields where lonely deer browse.
Down the heel in sloping grass blades
I find new born lambs springing
and a fence, and a sheep dog,
and a flea rises up, the nuisance
of a gnawing simplicity I miss so.
Fingers callous, the awkward scratch
a hen claws over my dirty mind.
I cough, dust lifts above lime,
my pen going wild in the barn
to leak milk from a stone if the sun
allows us one more day.

Aunt Mabel Talks About Adultery

Sally Green

Don't know why you have to go
and ask me such a question.

I don't even like the word. It's one of those
brutal sounds gets inside you churning
up feelings, even ones you didn't know
you owned. Like a plow tearing through
played-out land gone to seed.

And it makes no matter whether
its kin, or a dear friend
the pain of it all spreads quick
as prairie fire threatening everything
in its way. And that's all
I've got to say about it.

Down the Road a Bit in America

Bryce Milligan

If you didn't own a Ford back in the day then you likely didn't take those long rambling road-trip vacations to remote caverns or hidden canyons or desert meteor crash sites, and so there will not linger at the back of your memory a dusty adobe motel with honest-to-god tumble weeds and windmill water thick enough to chew, but rather the postcard visions of these same places, painted in back-alley New York studios where big sky sunsets and painted deserts came out just this side of psychedelic. But either way, whether the etched memory is real or second-hand illusion, now, a few miles down the road from one of America's more famous caverns, there is a rundown tourist court. . . . Probably, just down the road from every geographic or cultural oddity in the world there is some equivalent of the rundown tourist court—I mean, Lord, there's a souvenir shack on top of Mount Sinai—but in America, generally a mile or two down what was in the '30s a new two-lane blacktop but is now a pot-hole pocked, disintegrating back road half a mile or more off the smoothly sterile modern highway, up out of the landscape will rise some raggedy remnant of the days when being a tourist was a serious communal adventure, some L- or U-shaped building made of the very soil it stands on, lined with peeling, turquoise-painted door frames with illegible numbers, looking very much like some backwoods brothel except that you're in the wrong state for that and besides, only the goldenest of golden-hearted hookers would deign to make a warm and welcoming getaway of such a place—and there are not many of those ladies left (maybe there never were very many at all)—and with the wind whipping up a dust storm in the distance that looks like sundown before the Ragnarök, and your GPS spouting nonsense, and your cell phone that's texting "are you kidding?" to your every inquiry—then that place by the side of the road begins to have a certain appeal, and you begin to think of yourself as a hollow-souled wanderer about to meet Gabrielle Maple by the now-defunct gasoline pumps where she will be reading Françoise Villon and you will quote T.S. Eliot to her, or maybe its appeal is not Depression-era romanticism at all, but simply the exotic absence of neon, whatever, but you see a wavering light in the office window and a rusted "vacancy" sign that's creaking a soprano solo above the deep tenor hiss that is sand-blasting your windshield, and now you don't really decide, but your hands turn the wheel of themselves and set the brake and turn the key, and you wonder if there's coffee inside and just how gritty it is, and just how bad the scorpions in the shower will be, and whether the silhouette in the window can possibly match your imagination.

Itinerary

Jim Milstead

Here,
long ago,
the land rolled.
Crowds fled in panic.
Burnt into the matrix of the dark,
afterimages flared. Smoke settled on the city.
An abyss of stale air, a hint of dark
contagion dampening the spirit.

shutters open,
lenses search the waning light,
strive to catch crisp memories
as far below a canopy of sky
forces assemble in a collusion of silence.

The winds stir sails, to overflow. Pelicans dive,
their feathers scrape the white capped bay.
Soaring, they form a kite against the darkening air.
As the winds rise, the boat rides bull waves upon jade water.
To the west the bridge becomes an orange harp.
seines the sun's fire.

Beyond Lands End the headlands, pulled from the sea,
rise shear and shadowy. On Ocean Beach,
foam rushes to cover black sand. Flocks
of bubbles glisten, burst, and flow away.
Only a hint of Farralons far out,
monument to subduction, erosion, loss of identity.

San Francisco, a city newly risen. A city of the twinkied
excuse, the vigilante compulsion, the oxymoronic milieu,
summers of love, needled aspirations, hash piped fantasies.
A city of lost children searching for paradise.

Today the dawn lifts on a rubble
of thin old men not many manage,
some take advantage,
barter their unkempt dreams for small change.

In the arboretum the jaws of Venus gape,
while Mimosa shyly withdraws into itself.
Within the Palace Rodin's bronze sits in contemplation.
The dark aroma of a small North Beach Cafe invades
the senses, evokes the good life. Messages written
on mission walls scream their blind protest.

Somewhere sirens shriek, lights flicker,
horns utter annoying redundancies.
Sidewalk chess wars progress.
At the Exploratorium a frog leg twitches,
within the Tactile Dome, confusion reigns.

North above Market,
tall columns of concrete and glass
rasp the sky raw with excess.
Lithe men move hurriedly, nervously calm
viewing their virtues through veils of success,
finding them pleasing, appeasing their peers
in a rapid turnover of small ideas.

Nob Hill ladies sip their vermouth,
plasma drips into withered spirits,
armies of patrons gorge to overflow,
pastors decry the godless patterns of youth.

In the Audium dark echoes preside.
Within Lefty O'Douls devotees anchored
to ringside seats. Outside, ragged men
wrestle for stale scraps.

We are a microcosm, a city of Empire.
Pulsing to anomalous beats.
At the edge of a continent.

Milstead, con't.

A land of eternal hypothetical premise.

Forces gather in silent collusion,
gather to mass the next intrusion.

Busily immersed in busyness everywhere,
we are hardly aware of danger,
ignoring all that has gone before:
the sandstonedsubstrateslide
the glide towards oblivion,

the ever beckoning dark promise
of this bright city,

moving north in slow increments.

A True Bomb

Larry Crist

The two Johns sat watching the film rushes.

"Can I freshen your cocktail, John?" The younger of the two rose from where he was sitting.

"That would be nice, John. Thanks."

"Was that one olive, or two?"

"Better make it one. I need to watch my gut."

"Here you go, John."

"Thanks, John."

It was their little joke. No one else called them John. The man everyone called Mr. Ford sat in a large orange chair, an arm-reach from the the click-clack of the projector.

The other John, sipping a fresh martini, everybody everywhere recognized as the Duke. "This film has 'turkey' all over it. I wish you were directing it."

"I would never touch this tripe—you're miscast. Yul Brenner should be playing your part."

"Yul Brenner? He'll never carry a film. He's Broadway all-the-way."

"Well, you're all cowboy and all wrong for this picture."

"The Western is dead. Television has stolen our genre. I'm sure as hell not going to start going on TV—let Ronald Reagan do that—the putz."

"Well, I don't see you as the historic epic type. Dickie Burton you ain't."

"Hell." The Duke spit in a can he kept around for the purpose and reached for a Marlboro. He had done some print ads for Marlboro and never had to buy another pack as long as he lived.

"I mean, this pic is laughable. Your fans are going to drown it out, laughing. Like John Gilbert talking—this could ruin you."

"Jesus, maybe the studio will shelve it."

"Doubtful. They put too much money into it already. RKO is reeling. . . this could be the final nail in the coffin for them as well. Why in hell did you agree to do it?"

The Duke narrowed his gray eyes. "I don't know—promise you won't laugh?"

"No."

"They said they were going to give it to Brando if I turned it down."

"Ha... You know he's playing Napoleon right now, and just finished up Julius Caesar... hell, Brando'll play anything—he could play Genghis Khan standing on his head."

"Meaning what, I can't?"

"Well, we're viewing the results... You got an untried, inexperienced director. Brando would have fought for a better director, and script doctoring, too. Did you ever actually read the script?"

"Uh, not until it was too late. Hell, I've been fighting with that crazy wife of mine and working non-stop to pay for everything." Without looking away from the screen, Duke lit another cig off the one before.

"I especially enjoy where you and Pedro Armendariz ride all day, and that big tell-tale Utah monolith is still in the background by day's end."

"It's a pretty monolith."

"Don't I know it, I used it many times myself. 'Course that whole area was closed to us for awhile by the Army."

"Some underground testing as I understand it. I don't see what the big deal is, or was. It's gotta be good if it scares the Commies."

"Frightened the horses, too."

"Anyway, that was a couple years back and well over a hundred miles away—it's safe now, and we're safer 'cause we have a true bomb, one that the Soviet scum will respect."

"Well, you should know a true bomb when you see one. That Hayward woman still puttin' moves on you?"

"My god, you wouldn't believe it. She's worse than Marlene—this scene coming up... it's a medium shot, so you aren't seeing her hands, well, let me tell you, hers were busy. I didn't want to blow the shot, so I just let her fumble away, but it was pretty distracting all the same."

"You're a professional, Duke, no one ever said you weren't. They might not make the same claim for your acting, however."

"There—it's digs like that that have given me this... I don't know, Brando complex... what's his secret?"

"Different school. The difference being that he's gifted. He's also a major pain in the ass."

"Susan Hayward is a major pain in the ass, it don't mean she can act—anyway, I don't act—that's a sissy's game, I react."

"And it has served you well. Unfortunately, every time you try and *react* in this turkey, you're asked to talk as well. The script encroaches upon your every reaction. In short, you look like a fool."

"Damn it, Pappy, I know. I'll need to make another war movie just to save my rep. Why don't you direct me in another war movie, coach?"

"I tried. It was called World War Two—it ran for six years. You stayed home, and made, what? *The Fighting Seabees*, along with all the other 4-Fs."

"Aw, heck, you know I feel bad about that. The timing of that war was never good with my career. But I've devoted myself now to being a cold war warrior—you watch, there's a lot of war still to be fought, and I'm in the position with the right medium to help fight it."

"Playing Genghis Khan."

"After Genghis Khan. I'll redeem myself, you'll see—if this damn barbarian doesn't knock me out of the gate."

"Well, I was thinkin' of makin' another western, if I can get the project on track—it's called, *The Searchers*."

"Well, if you give it to me, you know I'll read it. Sounds kinda weak though."

"What do you mean?"

"Searching. . . I don't know, sounds—indecisive. *They Were Expendable*. Now there's a strong title."

"*The Conqueror* sounds strong too 'til you see the movie."

"*The Searchers*. . . mmm, yet it's kind of vulnerable. What are they searching for?"

"A girl is abducted by Comanches—it's about racism really. You'll see, it'll be a darn good picture. Don't think I'll shoot it in the shadow of that particular monolith however. That territory that's supposed to be 'outer Mongolia' looks played out to me."

"I had no problem with the background, it's what's in the foreground I disliked."

"Kinda looms over everything, like a mushroom cloud—HA!—I don't know, that's how things look when you only got one eye."

Ford re-lit his pipe. "Like a mushroom cloud, like that thing they were testing. . . how far away was that did you say?"

"A good day's ride, at least. It's safe—the Army said it was safe and that's good enough for me. It's got the Commies on the run. Joe McCarthy is routing them out in D.C. We got 'em in check in Korea. Hell, we should be pullin' outa there any time. And the French are fightin' in Indochina."

"I heard they called it a day. *Ceci ne marche pas.* Ike's sending in advisors. Bet we'll have to take up the slack."

"Well, nobody ever accused the French of being great soldiers. Hell, they don't even bathe regularly. Well, we've saved their ass before, reckon we can do it again." The Duke finished his drink and lit another cigarette. He sauntered back to the bar.

"'Bout time you made me another."

"Why, I was just about to call it a night. I have a 6 a.m. call."

"You'd let me drink alone. Bad enough you let me go to war by myself."

"Alright, but I gotta get some shuteye after this—the same?"

"You know it."

"*The Searchers*, eh? You're not going to give it to Brando if I turn it down?"

"You won't turn it down. You'll be champing at the bit."

"Searchers. . . racism? Why can't westerns just be about good versus evil anymore?"

"'Cause not everybody wants to see *Randy Rides Alone* again and again—you'll like it. They'll forget all about Genghis Whatshisname."

"Well, I'll do it for you, Pappy. I just hope they don't cast another queer along side me that I'll have to beat up. That kind of thing never looks good."

"So, Rock and Monty are out?"

"Please."

"It'll be your best part since *The Ringo Kid*, you'll love it."

"Wish we could do something to counter Communism—this Arthur Miller guy, Dashiell Hammett, even Bogart... they're all soft on Commies, quick to make excuses too."

"Well, we'll see. Racism might prove a pretty pertinent subject."

"Hell, they've integrated baseball, and the Army, what more do they want? It's Communism that's the scourge of the age. It's everywhere." Having handed Ford a fresh martini with one olive, Duke lit a new Marlboro. "Goddamn Commies, it eats at me like cancer."

Just then the rushes ended. The celluloid flapped franticly. Ford reached up with his one good arm and switched it off. The room went black. Both men waited for the other to hit the light switch, but neither moved. Perhaps they had forgotten where it was. The two Johns continued to drink in the dark.

Author note: The Conqueror, *released in 1956, was filmed in Nevada in 1954 two years after a nuclear bomb had been tested in the same area. Two decades later, at least 91 people involved in* The Conqueror, *including John Wayne, had died from cancer. No telling how many Indian and Mexican extras died as well. John Ford served six years in the military. In World War Two he was badly wounded losing one eye as well as the use of one arm. John Wayne managed a 4-F rating, and made several dozen war movies, as well as his stock'n trade western.*

After an Evening Performance of the Nutcracker at Boston's Opera House

Jon D. Lee

It was wicked good
especially when they brought out all the little kids in their fancy dresses
and had 'em run around the stage bangin' on drums
and I liked how the clock in the back was actually a real clock
and not one of those painted-on things that look fake
and the part in the middle where they had that big Christmas tree
that just grew and grew until it hit the ceiling was pretty neat
must of done it by wires or gears under the floor
at least that part you couldn't tell how it was done
unlike when that sleigh came out of the roof and carried 'em all off
that part you could just see the wires
that coulda been done better
but for the most part it was wicked good
what I don't understand is how this is a show for kids
I mean there were tons of 'em onstage and the audience was filled with 'em
and most of the time they were even pretty quiet
but some of them dancers weren't wearing a whole lot
or exactly leaving a whole lot to the imagination if you know what I mean
like that guy who played the Nutcracker and came out wearing that big mask
that guy was only wearing a little pair of white tights jumping around like that
and stuff bounces around you know
like when he was doing all those leaps and things and twirling around
it was pretty hard not to look
I mean I know it was supposed to be pretty and all
and I'm not gay
but every time that guy moved all I could think about was junk and ass
and it kinda ruined the show

The *Notorious* Story

Andrea Carter

Who would have thought Brazil
had a white sun, the whale stomach
sheen of the FBI station chief
lying beached in his bed
spreading caviar on white bread
disdaining the daughter's reputation,
and her black heart will let her
marry a Nazi to go undercover.

The job makes her cry gray tears
across white cheeks after she drinks
the black poison in the black coffee,
and Dr. Anderson is off to the mountains
to mine uranium; the war is not over.

Of course, at the time, the world works
in *chiaroscuro,* and it's easy to see
white canyons and black suns, besides
Brazil is all the way over and upside down.
With too much whiskey and champagne
and racehorses, you'd be wearing
your shadow like a shield, like a plate
of armor. Finally, when Ingrid Bergman

escapes the mansion of ash
and fascism, as her fur coats melts
into the ocean, the grand dame mother-
in-law no longer able to light white ideas
for Ingrid's black death. I wonder, did they
get away, Cary Grant's FBI prince and his
secret agent squeeze, did they escape to
Recife or Manaus, or did they make
their way across the border into color?

Fairy Tale

Elizabeth Thrall

Dusty volumes smile on their shelves

Patiently waiting to be picked up

Characters sleep in their pages, waiting

For a reader to take them home.

Sunlight dances in the window under

The old wooden sign bearing the name of

The place where love can be found

Battles can be fought and won

Princesses marry the commoner

And fruit should never be eaten.

When you enter this place remember

Some are old, be gentle

Some are new, make friends

And never ever listen to a step-mother.

swooping owl—

for a moment the moon

not quite full

—*Seren Fargo*

Responsible Parties

Norman L. Green

Dream, home, 5:48 am

Return to the urban landscape that mixes Vancouver with Houston, Little Rock and Bellingham. This time there are many people I know from the waking world.

I have moved my printing operation from one section of town into another. Equipment, not yet organized, so I have difficulty when a woman shows up needing me to work with a terrible piece of paste-up art—torn, irregular shapes scotch-taped to a piece of light card stock. Somehow I am expected to duplicate it and have all of the finished pieces in the exact jagged patterns presented in the art. She warns me that we have done it before, and she expects the same results. She needs them for a big street party event that will occur this night. When she leaves, I take her art apart to make something more executable. I end up losing the torn bits, and then I lose interest.

By now, nightfall, everyone in the town works in frenzied preparation for the big event. I get dragooned by a group of caterers to prepare carts full of art food: *hors d'oeuvres* shaped like little creatures. As we send out each cart, another returns with dirty dishes that I must clean in order that we might re-fill them with fresh food. The process slows down as the event, on the south side of the city, winds to a close.

Ray comes in to tell us to shut down for the night, that he has arranged for us to stay in a house on the edge of downtown.

One of the women with whom I have been working needs to use the ladies room, but this building has none. I remember that there is one in my old shop, which stands across the street from our kitchen. I still have the keys so offer to escort her through the crowds so that I might unlock the glass door and let her in. We make our way through the night street and the remainder of the street party people.

When we get to the corner where my former shop had stood, we cross under a police cordon tape. The building has been turned into a record store by my old friend Gene. When we reach the entrance, we find that the glass doors have been smashed. The woman I have accompanied crunches across the cubes of shattered glass and through the darkened shop to the back corner where she will find the ladies room.

I stand guard at the entrance when two police officers, who wear dark blue uniforms from the 1950s, approach me to question my presence. I tell them that I have a key to the premises, and that I know the new owner of the shop. I show them the key, though there seems to be no door in which to test it. The woman reappears and we are allowed to leave without incident.

Many old friends, visitors from out-of-town, have gathered at a bungalow, the house that Ray has borrowed for the night. All of the rooms are arranged off of a central corridor. The bedrooms all feel as though they have been recently occupied. About a dozen of us will stay the night. I open a drawer in one of the dim, back bedrooms—reminds me of our third from last home in Little Rock—and borrow a red t-shirt to use as sleep-wear. In the main room, people have rolled out sleeping bags. Voices are low as people catch up with each other's lives at this short reunion.

Morning comes and the place is in disarray, clothes and blankets piled on the floors. People grab cups of coffee in the back kitchen.

Ray returns with some distressing news: "This is house number 1028—we were supposed to stay at 2810."

"Then whose house is this?" I ask.

Ray shrugs, "I don't know, but they just pulled into the driveway."

"Isn't this a movie plot?" *

Ray mugs an I'm-a-gettin'-out-of-here grimace and disappears out the front door.

I rush around the house and return things to their drawers. I take off the red t-shirt and add it to a laundry pile in one of the children's rooms. No one should notice one more shirt. I plan to leave in hopes that our visit goes undetected. But when I go outside, I have second thoughts.

Many neighbors have turned-out to welcome the returning family. The man and the woman are the patriarch and matriarch of the black community. To the north side of the house the couple has pulled their car into the driveway. This side of the house has a hillside that drops off sharply, so as I look over the edge to see the home owners, a full-grown tree stands below me. The tree's wide smooth branches are filled with the neighborhood children. One girl looks up at me with alarm on her face. I decide to stay and face the music, to make my apologies, and to explain the confusion of the accidental guests.

I cannot approach the man and woman as they are surrounded by many from the town celebrating their return. Away from the crowd, one of the family's old and dear friends walks on a paved path with a younger man. They discuss the upcoming mayoral election. The man wears a beautifully tailored suit of ivory with burnt orange pin-stripes and matching hat. His sunglasses have wide lenses and thick gold frames. He speaks confidently of his likely election. I walk up and ask him to introduce me to the owners of the house, explaining that I need to make my apology. He comforts me with a graveled voice and a hand on my shoulder.

Inside, the house is again filled with people, but now they speak in full voice—not out-of-town guests, but extended family to the owners. Some heads turn to see the only white man in the building. Most smile and nod as I pass on my way back through the house to a great room where the couple receives their visitors.

The man who will be the next mayor introduces me to the matriarch, a woman in her middle sixties with a proud round face and coffee-with-cream complexion. She wears a salmon toned crepe dress and a green scarf. I tell her that I would like to make an apology to her and to her husband.

She calls him over. He is a handsome man of great dignity—I fully understand the respect that these two are given by the community—he asks that we three take seats that face each other. His voice has impossibly rich resonance. In a choking voice, I explain that my friends and I have accidentally invaded their home, believing that it belonged to out-of-town friends. The woman lays a gentle hand on my knee while he places one on my shoulder.

"It's alright" he says. "I too have made my mistakes—I remember being told 'Victor, Victor, Victor.'" He repeats, "'Victor, Victor, Victor.'"

Still choking, but less violently, I am anxious to hear what advice he was given and am reminded of the torn pieces of paper from the first woman's paste-up.

It is actually the story behind the making of the Laurel & Hardy short Big Business– *The Hal Roach Studios paid to partially destroy a private home as part of the film's plot. As they finished the film, the actual owners of the home returned to inform the departing crew that they had come to the wrong address. Expensive restitution had to be paid.*

Dinner at Deborah's

Shelley Muzzy

"Down, Heidi, Bea! Get down!" Two huge gray Weimaraners bounced and skittered, ignoring Deborah's sharp commands. A cigarette followed her arm movements, unlocking the gate, pushing the unruly dogs away as I shrunk back. Deborah's long blond hair fell over one shoulder, and her black stretch pants peeked below a simple black tunic spatter painted with parts of our dinner. In her chunky black mules, she conveyed an air of elegant dishevelment, skirting the edges of what might be considered slovenly. Dinner at Deborah's was about to begin.

A large oval rug woven by Deborah's husband Lee dominated the center of the rustic 19th century style log cabin. Mismatched antique wooden chairs lined wall space or stood in small groups. A large circular oak dining table stood in the center of the rug. Off to the sides, an armoire in faded blue paint held the stereo. Antique wooden trunks stacked like a pyramid served as extra shelving. It would be an understatement to say Deborah had a knack for Shabby Chic. Books and candles were arrayed on the mantle of a river rock fireplace. Both Deborah and her husband were college professors.

On a south facing wall hung a portrait I assumed to be Deborah's father in a sack jacket and slouched fedora and opposite, near the fireplace, hung a painting of the house and grounds in muted fuzzy oils rendered by a well-known local artist. In a conversation many years after our first encounter, Deborah revealed the origins of man in the hat. As a young stewardess for Pan Am, she spotted the oil portrait in a silent auction at a St. Vincent de Paul thrift store in Greenwich Village. She placed a bid in an envelope, never thinking that it would be hers for a meager $100. Though the $100 at the time was dear, she proudly carried the portrait home and he was affectionately known everafter as "Vinnie."

An ancient enameled sink tilted drunkenly in a rough-hewn cabinet in Deborah's kitchen. The knotty pine walls had darkened from countless years of wood smoke. An antediluvian stove listed slightly to one side in a far corner, oozing a faint smell of gas. The oven snapped and creaked when fired up. The burners hissed and sputtered as Deborah manipulated pots and pans over a surface half the size of a normal range. The door of the oven required Deborah's deft manipulation to close.

Jutting into the center of the kitchen space from under a low window facing the backyard was a long uneven wooden table. On plank shelving beneath it, a stack of hand-turned wooden bowls teetered next to blackened pots and pans. Knives, cloves of garlic, cheese graters, parcels of this, bundles of that, bottles of wine, bowls of salt and packages of cheese and butter covered the surface.

From the small multi-paned windows over the sink, towering shrub roses wrestled with gnarled rhododendrons for space in the unkempt garden surrounding the house and grounds like the briar guarding Sleeping Beauty's castle. The Weimaraners, ears flopping and tongues lolling lunged through the house, barking furiously at every new knock on the door. Their long hard toenails clicked like castanets across the wooden floors as they skidded to a stop by their bowl of water directly under a bag suspended from a high cupboard door. Every trip to the garbage bag involved a delicate dance around the dogs and through the pool of water collecting around their dish.

The partial wall separating the kitchen from the dining area was an open cupboard filled with an encyclopedia of exotic ingredients. Deborah was a bargain shopper, haunting the dollar stores and discount houses. From the jars, boxes and bottles in her prodigious stash, Deborah created feasts fit for the gods.

The first night we ate at Deborah's I sat in awe, watching her intricate performance, darting from kitchen to table, keeping up a dialog with new guests, and with me. I can't remember what we had, but that dinner, and every other one I ate at her house over the years was prefaced by the conspiratorial admonition, "Darling, it's nothing really. I haven't a clue what I'm making. Now it's not fancy, so you'll just have to make the best of it!"

Along with Deborah's eternal search for a new house, she also searched for the best napkins and the most unique place servings. She corrected me continuously on the placement of knives, forks and spoons until it became a joke among the dining regulars and I finally flat out refused to even try setting the table. A mutual friend shared her observations with me years later that in the plays she directed, Deborah was an amazing set dresser. When she got it right her sets would have a sumptuousness even if it was a fairly simple set. To some extent her home was a set, marked by a constantly changing parade of furniture and props.

In the midst of what seemed like indifferent chaos, an offbeat table formality ensued. Deborah's attention to detail from place setting to wine selection created an ambient atmosphere for conversation and manners. I recall the dark blue Bennington spongeware from Vermont, Deborah used at that first dinner party I attended. The dishes were irregular and coarse in an early American style, and remained among my favorites. Years later when she gave me a few mismatched pieces, I heard a rumor that the bulk of the set had been broken when she threw them at Lee in a drunken rage. I never saw that Deborah. I saw an eccentric, direct, inquisitive Deborah, sometimes intimidating, but never the alcoholic harpy. I did notice that the Bennington dishes were gone without comment at a party, replaced with antique white-wear that she scoured from several second hand stores.

Stopping occasionally to smoke, leaning in the low-framed doorway to the dining room, Deborah periodically contributed a little verbal fuel to the conversational fire. She casually slid appetizers and apologies onto the table, rushing out of the room and tossing instructions over her shoulder. I still have her succulent antipasto recipe; tuna, carrots, cauliflower, olives and anchovies in a spicy oily tomato sauce, no amounts given, done to taste. There were plates of roasted red peppers and cappers in olive oil, bruschetta with homemade aioli, tapenades and marinated goat cheese, julienned peppers and onions reduced in butter to a caramelized decadence, anchovy butter that beguiled even an anchovy hater like me.

Because the guests knew these dinners would be wonderful, the wines we brought were wonderful too. We oohed and ahhed and smacked our lips over bottles of dry merlots and spicy Shiraz, bold zinfandels and an occasional French Bordeaux. Cabernets and rustic Chianti were preceded early in the evening by chardonnays that whispered of oak and butter, and after dinner fine port was served with cigars and coffee.

Dinner frequently began with a pasta dish. This is where Deborah excelled. In the summer, she served it with fresh tomatoes diced and soaked in olive oil, garlic and basil. In the colder months, tomatoes with garlic and basil were roasted in a heavy cast iron baking dish until slightly black, mashed with a wooden spoon and stirred into hot pasta. Nothing went to waste.

"Hand me that leftover cheese. Let's put this butter in." She tossed in the uneaten appetizers, grabbed a pinch of salt, twisted a grind of pepper and threw it in a bowl.

"Will you take this in, dear?"

Deborah followed with small blocks of Parmesan perched atop a grater.

Between her musings about the dinner itself, there were interminable questions and comments delivered in her throaty inquisitive voice. She always gave the impression she was listening intently. And she was.

Main dishes were bouillabaisse, osso bucco with oxtails ordered from the meat counter at Larry's Market in Seattle, thick steaks barely seared on the barbecue, lobster tails with bowls of butter and lemon, fresh salmon with marinade and an extemporaneous salsa of bits of fruit and chilis. Courses from Russia, from Turkey, from Spain, were all cooked with her own touches, never straight from a cookbook, never with a recipe. No one was a vegetarian at Deborah's, though there was always every sort of food to allow for any idiosyncrasy of palate. Butter sat at either end of the table, softened and mushed into small bowls, salt was served in cellars conveniently placed at intervals, and each new offering precipitated a new toast, a fresh bottle of wine, all with the table commentary uninterrupted except for exclamations of, "Delicious! Lee, could you bring more bread, more butter, does anyone want water? It is good, isn't it?' Deborah's smile lit her face as she leaned toward you and chuckled at another successful dinner.

As I became more comfortable with Deborah, I stood at her side, watching, learning, trying to cull her secrets. It was all in the details. If cheeses had not been served as an appetizer, cheese and fruit were the prelude to dessert. At Christmas there was special ripe Stilton. There was runny brie, ripe, creamy camembert, sharp piquant cheshires and deliciously aged blues. Fruit was seasonal except for the ripe pears served as a treat in the middle of winter when it would be most appreciated. The cheeses were arrayed on a wooden platter and the fruit came sliced or whole in bowls. People took turns peeling, slicing, and handing around chunks.

Evenings ended with dessert and coffee. Perhaps an almond cake, or cheesecake so light and delicate it seemed to float off the fork, a rich moist torte made with chocolate and nuts, baked pears in wine sauce, trifles swimming in liqueurs, simple fruit and custard tarts, fresh berry or apple cobblers and homemade ice cream, or topped with fresh cream whipped by hand with a whisk, never something as crude as an electric mixer. Lee ground the coffee beans in an ancient grinder attached to the wall of the kitchen, and an array of mismatched cups appeared on the table with small pitchers of real cream and a bowl of sugar. The smell of those beans and the brewing coffee made my heart content. It signaled the end of a wonderful evening full of conversation punctuated by courses of food.

But it wasn't just the food.

There was something that made her dinners special. It was the atmosphere, the cooking and blending of diverse souls that seemed to bring out the very best in everyone, just like a savory stew in which each ingredient contributes the right note. Conversations ranged over topics as divergent as female circumcision to auto mechanics. Writers talked about works in progress, theater people talked about plays, gossip abounded. One night, a writer who had worked as a transvestite dancer in Las Vegas graphically demonstrated how he tied up his genitals in order to wear tights. Another woman just back from the Middle East shared stories about hauling milk for Iraqi children across the dessert from Syria during the first blockade. Deborah regaled us with stories from her days as an airline stewardess, living in Greenwich Village, seeing belly dancers and jazz musicians in dusky, musty cabarets. She told us about living in Panama when she was in the military. In the blowsy woman before me, I could see her, thin and ravishing, her long blond hair impeccably coiffed, strutting down the aisle of an airplane dispensing drinks and pillows.

Over cigars and brandy, cigarettes and wine we discussed diets and sexual depravity and English literature. We argued politics, semantics, religion and historical oddities, poets, playwrights, authors and arcane mysteries. We gossiped about the rich and famous, the poor and obscure. We sang Brecht, discussed Leni Riefensthal, German Expressionism, Dada, Antonin Artaud, Diego Rivera, and Woody Guthrie. We laughed over alligators in the sewers, discussed the massacre of Chinese mine workers, shuddered at tales bizarre and depraved. All opinions were honored and aired. In those hours we each felt intelligent and dignified and special. We felt alive.

Art is about a vision of the finished product and then working backwards. It is practice and attention to detail and orchestration. Deborah worked hard to make every dinner a memorable event, but in truth, there was no hint of hard work in it. Every movement of her delicate and complex dance, from invitation to farewell, was done with generosity and grace. Without love and attention, dinner is just food and dinner parties are a chore. Every invitation to dinner at Deborah's was a gift. I felt as honored as if I had been called to wait upon the Queen. I miss her cooking, her conversation, and the celebration of life in her gatherings. I will not meet her like again.

While from the Kitchen Wafts the Scent of Something Burning on the Stove

Rosemerry Wahtola Trommer

Flipping through the magazine
I find an ad for my life. They are selling it
at a discount—20 percent off if you call
this month. The children are smiling.
Their clothes are clean, their hair
brushed, and in the picture they
are picking up their yard toys, laughing.
My husband, very handsome, smiles at me adoringly,
and I smile back. My teeth are perfect,
though a tad yellow, my smile real.
My Volvo, sea foam with tan seats,
must have just been through the car wash,
and it shines in the golden light beside the garden,
which is weeded and hoed. The lettuce,
already up, is thinned, and at least
from this distance there are no aphids
in the leaves. In the upper left,
the solar eclipse has just begun, and
there is a sense that the birdsong
in the picture has just quieted
so that one might better hear
the hushed rush of the river, not pictured.
In the lower right corner
an asterisk buried in the yellow tulips
snuggles up against
some very fine print that mentions
how the picture is merely a suggestion.
I know that the next four pages
will be black and white text, 8 point,
with testimonies from my friends,
my parents, my therapists. They will

divulge all the secrets I tried for years
to hide under my skin. Six columns
of side effects: A predilection toward
weeping in public. Inability to remember
important dates. Addictions to Diet Pepsi, and
listening to a cappella versions of Lady Gaga.
Aversion to going to sleep. Perfectionism. Erroneous
belief in an ability to mind read. Decades
of low self esteem. There is more. I laugh
at the disclaimer about lack of boundaries
and refusal to see it as a problem. Oh please.
I flip the page to read an article on the Science of Nothing,
but halfway through the first paragraph
I flip back to the ad, take a slug of Diet Pepsi,
and shout at the kids to stop bickering
so I can make a phone call. I'm ready to offer full price.

Dark

Laurel Rust

In the quiet of morning
I wait for coffee water to boil
and for words to shape themselves
in the strange box of myself

and finally give up,
and write a letter,
because I need to imagine
someone
opening it.

Moving

Dayna Patterson

We begin the relentless sorting
with books, measuring each
in the balance of our desire

to keep them and our aversion to shift
heavy things. Some are old
friends, too dear to leave behind

despite their weight. Dust is a fur
on others. We toss
those in a pile destined

for a thrift store. Some objects
are more difficult to assess.
The ottoman, for example,

is filthy, a map with continents
of spill stains, capitals marked
by wandering felt tips and ball points.

The dirt, however, makes it easier
to kick off muddy shoes (or not)
and rest sweaty feet.

This roasting pan, a gift
from the wedding, we've used once
in eight years and four moves.

And what about the bins
of baby clothes, the bassinet,
the crib with all its bolts and springs

rusting like my womb,
long empty despite hope?
How about the toothbrush I bought

Patterson, con't.

with too much money, which led
to the longest fight we've had?
Should we pack the pain

of the words we flung at each other,
blunt weapons bruising not-thick-enough
skin? It might clash with the knickknacks,

the harmony of the living room's
chintz and houndstooth.
And our religion,

the faith that sprouted for us both
when we were seedlings,
but has begun to wither.

Maybe we leave those potted plants
on the porch, like an accident,
shedding pale petals in the wind.

One Hundred Words For Hanging On Your Kitchen Wall

Tony Curtis

Twenty years from now
Somebody's child will ask
Where the words hanging
By the back door came from.
Then somebody's hands will take
Down this poem from where it's hung
For years, unnoticed, and read
The words to the tosselled-haired child.
"Dear one, you who sit in the kitchen
Where I once sat and laughed
With a small gathering of friends.
If you go out now into the garden
You will see the trees I looked on,
The grass I walked over. I wish
You could have been there that night.
I would have read a poem just for you."

a clutch of eggs

in a robin's nest

I think

of Mom's love

for turquoise.

— *Andrew Shattuck McBride*

Holding My Mother's Hand

Jon D. Lee

My parents and I:
walking home late from a Christmas party,
the ghosts of fruitcake and wine
forming small wreaths in our breath.
I have not seen my parents since Spring,
and because of this,
and because the lights twinkle around us like Technicolor gods,
and because the course of our steps
reveals that we have had
perhaps
too much wine,
I take my mother's hand,
wrapping her smaller fingers in mine to steady our pace.
"This is nice," she says.
"You haven't held my hand since you were a kid."
Which makes me smile, and,
thinking of the lines we draw between ourselves and others,
I grip my mother's hand the more tightly,
holding on to what I can
as we move into the night.

Ma Chérie Amour

Janet Bergstrom

Ma chérie! said Miss Dos Santos. "You must visit me in Paris. Perhaps your parents will allow you to come next summer?"

I knew my parents couldn't afford to send me to Paris, and I cried when Miss Dos Santos left to return to her hometown. We wrote letters to one another for a while, but that soon fizzled. Although I never saw her again, she left behind with me an indelible yearning to learn French and travel the world.

Thirty years after Miss Dos Santo's awakening words, I traveled to Paris with my 16-year-old daughter Anna, a budding Francophile. Paris enchanted us in the ways only Paris can. We climbed the Eiffel Tower to look across the expanse of the ancient architecture, walked along the River Seine, toured Notre Dame Cathedral, viewed master art at Louvre, walked along Champs-Élysées to the Arc de Triomphe, and strolled through Luxembourg and Tuileries Gardens that were pruned and plucked into perfection. While sitting on park benches we ate cheap *Croque-monsieur* sandwiches because we were too excited to stop for long meals. When we took time to enjoy leisurely dinners, another kind of perfection melted on our palates–buttery sauces, flaky pastries, and other fussy preparations.

"*Votre fille est très douce. Est-ce qu'elle est toujours si douce avec vous?*" Asked a man sitting next to us in a park.

"Yes," I agreed. "My daughter is very sweet–most of the time, and I am fortunate she enjoys traveling with me."

After ten days of Parisian bliss we traveled south by train to Nice to take French lessons during the mornings for the next three weeks. Afternoons and weekends were free for explorations.

The humid French Riviera weather greeted us when we arrived in the city. Whizzing around hordes of summer visitors, a taxi delivered us to the University of Nice dormitories where Anna and I were each assigned a single room. From there we would sleep, eat meals and go to classes with other students who were scheduled to arrive throughout the day. Soon the dormitory came alive with hundreds of international students. English was the common language which unfortunately didn't force much French from Anna or me outside of our classes.

That first evening taking dinner in the cafeteria, I discovered most students were in the 15-25 age range. I was one of the few matronly students. I met two age-appropriate teachers named Laura and Wendy who were from Boston, Massachusetts, and another mother named Ananda from Nicaragua. The four of us became an instant clique.

As the crowd of young people eyed one another and the room swirled with hormones, my adult acquaintances and I found seats together for an orientation. Afterwards, the directors gathered us for a jaunt to the center of Nice to take us on a short walking tour. It was beyond my bedtime, but when in Nice, do as the *Niçoise* do, right?

The center of Old Town Nice where the language classes would meet the next day was filled with crowds. Active children, parents pushing strollers, tottering elders with walkers and canes, tourists holding maps and draped with backpacks and bags, uninhibited lovers embracing and kissing oblivious to their surroundings, and people murmuring in different languages–all meandered throughout the maze of cobblestone walkways. Beneath the street lamps were cafes surrounded by large pots of scented roses, orchids, and lavender mixed with banana palms and other luxuriant tropical plants. Patrons sat laughing, eating, sipping on drinks and enjoying the balmy evening. The scene resembled Van Gogh's famous painting, Cafe Terrace.

"This place is lively for 11:00 at night on a Sunday."

"Most people along the Mediterranean take a siesta during the hottest part of the afternoon, and then socialize late at night," said Laura.

We walked toward the sea among Belle Epoch hotels adorned with frescos, moldings and more flowers tumbling from grilled balconies. The Promenade des Anglais, curvied in a half-moon around Baie des Anges, hummed with walkers, skaters, teenagers, and more lovers walking arm-in-arm, all against the backdrop of the Mediterranean Sea lapping in scalloped waves along the shoreline.

Anna took my arm. "Oh Mom, this is the most amazing place in the world!" she crooned in my ear. "Thank you so much for bringing me here." She introduced me to Paulo, Sven, Sayori, Abdulla, and Bianca–all gorgeous, young, unsupervised and, judging from their chunky gold jewelry, rich. "Mom, I want to go out clubbing tonight. The drinking age is 16! Isn't that fantastic! You don't mind, do you?"

In that moment I realized, Nice–a paradise for a 16-year-old from Smalltown, America—was hell for the parent of the 16-year-old from the same place. Thrust into this delicate situation, I didn't want to slam the door on Anna's appreciation and sweetness, but I didn't want her to go out with these international strangers to clubs in downtown Nice. I opted for the mean mom approach. "I absolutely do mind and you will absolutely not go out to clubs and drink alcohol!"

Naturally, this response aroused the not-so-sweet-side of Anna's personality.

"Mu–ther!" she hissed at me. "Why not?"

"I wouldn't dream of letting you go to bars at home, and you wouldn't dream of asking to go to bars. You know it, and I know it."

"You're being a hypocrite! You said you want me to be exposed to other cultures." She gave me a look that could have ignited a forest fire in a rain storm. "In case you've forgotten, Mu–ther, we're not in *Smalltown* anymore. Please let me go. They're really nice."

"No."

"I'm not a child. Don't you trust me?"

I gave her the cliché answer, "Of course I trust you, Darling, but it's the others that concern me. You've just met them."

I forced her to come with me, while the other kids went out. I knew I was screwed, though. Three weeks of hauling her back for her bedtime every night would be like fighting alone in a war zone. I knew myself at her age, and I knew my parental authority versus gorgeous, international young people in this cosmopolitan Mediterranean city–was not a match. Still, I wanted to hang on to my authority for a while longer, but I had no idea how to handle the situation. I thought about packing up and leaving with Anna, but then I'd be punished too. My hard earned salary had financed the trip. What's a mother to do? I wondered. I didn't sleep well that night, trying to come up with a reasonable solution–some sort of assertion of control over my woman/child.

The next night, after dinner, Anna stretched, yawned, and said, "I think I'll go to bed."

I was immediately suspicious. I smiled and said, "Let's walk to our rooms together. Do you have a good book to read?"

"Oh, yes. I want to study my French, too. We went upstairs arm in arm. "Good-night, Mommy, *Je t'aime.*" She pecked my checks back and forth, French-style.

Anna went inside. I waited a few seconds, and then went back downstairs. As predicted, minutes later, Anna appeared, dressed to conquer, made up, and ready to sneak to Old Town Nice to do who-knows-what with her new friends.

"Mom!" she gasped when she saw me. "I thought you went to bed!"

"And I thought you went to bed!" I gave her a look that could have ignited a forest fire in a rain storm.

"I'm not tired!" Then she slumped in a chair and moaned, "Oh Mom, don't ruin my fun!"

"I'm not here to ruin your fun, Anna. And I don't want you to ruin mine. Do you understand what a difficult situation this is for me?"

"But Mom! You always worry. What could happen? I promise I won't drink anything but coke."

"C'mon, Anna, I'm not that naive."

"Well, I won't drink a lot. Besides, you let me take sips from your wine or beer."

I sighed. I knew that I needed to call upon my faith in her, and hoped that my years of dedicated parenting would see her through this unscathed. Possibly against my better judgment, I had to let her go. "Convince me that I should allow this," I challenged her. I liked this parenting tip a friend had taught me. I used it often and Anna always dreamed up more stipulations for herself than I would have, and then she had to obey her self-imposed rules, rather than mine.

She sighed. "I'll be back by 1:00 a.m., I'll knock on your door when I get back, I'll take plenty of money for a cab, I'll not be alone with strangers or boys, I'll make sure I have the address, I won't drink more than a sip or two, and I'll make safe choices."

That about covered it for me. I granted her permission, and hoped for the best. Before she left though, I warned her with the only applicable threat I could come up with under the circumstances. "If you break any of these rules you've set up for yourself, I promise you, that without a doubt, I will show up on the beach, walk up to you and your friends, and I will be topless. We're not in Smalltown, anymore. You know I'll do it. Don't push your luck."

She didn't push her luck, and I didn't have to follow through with my threat.

I don't know everything that happened during our visit in Nice, and I don't want to know. I enjoyed her new friends who called me Mom. We left three weeks later, both of us enriched and experienced in more ways than we expected.

a sericeous leaf

between my fingertips—

the way he speaks to me

—*Seren Fargo*

Leaving for Two Weeks

Nancy Takacs

For J

You unlock the cinnamon ferns, chickadees,
unlock the gold centers and quiet moth wings,
unlock the wish of entire, unlock *skim and hum*.

The sky a quilt-wheel, yesterday a mirror of hemlock.
You want the day of peacock chants,
a whip-poor-will that used to call from our elderberry.

You have that farmhouse aura inside skyscraper.
You were right about Perfect. But then
the edges have aroused denim.

I've filled up on strawberry and chive,
the crush of hull and stem almost unnerving.

I have your yellow flannel still in my back seat.
When I get back, you'll wear it on a porch
where they let you smoke.

Vanilla and lavender tapioca some night,
mock meat balls in rum.

You know how to rest the stems of asters,
you know when to bring
the blue hydrangeas in.

By The Wood Stove:
Under Leaves & Clouds

Tony Curtis

The first day of winter.
I am out in the yard
Chopping wood for the fire.
Beyond the hedge
The world has gone grey –
The island is full of sorrows.

I look back through the trees,
Through the quiet yellows
Of another November evening.
The woman I love, have always loved,
Stands by our back door.
Above her, the sky is clear blue.

On the radio the weatherman
Says there will be storms
By morning. But I don't think so.
And if there is? Well, then we can
Just sit by the wood stove
And talk about the clouds.

Lovers

Alan Cohen

When I hear about the cricket player
divorcing his wife, who
he married over the phone
after seeing her pictures online,
that weren't really her pictures…

I think about how we stand together
in the field in early April,
nothing needed to be said,
breathing the same fecund air
while holding each other's hand,
as the woodcock spirals against
the dappled sky and
plummets toward his lover

Botanical

Samuel Green

Maybe, at some stage, love includes kneeling
in dungarees beside the long-time belovéd
at a stem of Queen Anne's Lace, taking the time
to dig up a portion of the root, peel it
for the carroty smell, point out the umbels
that form a cup like the nest of a small bird,
a single central flower the red of a ruby, or a drop
of the queen's own blood, how the leaves are like lace.

And maybe love includes kneeling again alongside
a stalk of Yarrow near where the neighbor's goats
are tied, the tiny white clusters of blossoms different,
you tell him, one old hand guiding the tips of his
fingers to the shape of the leaves, their give &
bending—*plumajillo*, *"soft feathers,"*—telling the tale
of Achilles tending the hurts of his warriors
with a clever poultice. *Staunchweed*, you say. *Woundwort*.

And maybe this long love contains the nearly certain
knowledge that the belovéd, though he vows this time
to remember, might, in a week, mistake one plant
for the other as he has for more than forty years,
such love tenacious as any weed we might describe,
but cannot always name.

The Physics of Beauty

William O'Daly

Standing on the back patio we want to fly like dragons
into the night, and we see Quetzal's red eyes
flashing at the far edge of the meadow
where earlier that day we came upon
an abandoned encampment among the oaks,
a tattered couch and rusted bedsprings—
it was a summer spent swimming with hobos
and watching chickens jiggle
in the Canada moonlight,
you in your restless sleep, needing only
mystical monkey power
to land in Spain or Greece,
to take the high road to Paris
or Hanga Roa, to Venus crossing the desert
and talking with cows.

You are hopelessly in love
with the world and you know it.
You are in love with your dog,
with the random and deep song,
with Eminem's passion and the fierceness of Adele,
seeking a world that converges
in absolute best, calling the green bell
of your expanding solitude, the imagined real.
You stand against the violence of the sun,
against the demolition of the rain,
wanting no one left to loneliness—
your love expands with the universe,
your suffering is everyone's.

Together our memories will navigate
the harsh syllables and the salt,
the eddy and occasional ease,
the asphodels and mind. We will persevere

O'Daly, con't.

in truth or bitterness,
and hold each galaxy together
in a wash of darkness or an eyelid of light.

The day will come when, seeing
and caring, you will follow your road
far from here and let the night carry you.
Wherever you go rest your head
as though you are home,
and I will do the same.

Time Out of Mind

Mikel Vause

for Janis

Blue eyes
Set so wind blown
Hair the color of autumn wheat

Alive in sunlight
A smile brought
By nothing particular

A bird song
A lone sprig of Indian
paintbrush
Orange in the powder-green
sage

A grandchild's laugh
Or a gopher snake warming in the sun
On a cool Utah July morning

Your mysterious smile
In its beginnings
Rises from hidden well-
springs

A half a world away
Kathmandu
My dirty magical place

In a memory flash
This reaction to the present
From past's vales

Vause, con't.

All experience linked
Co-mingled like curry and
coriander
Like sage and juniper.

4/11/2011 Kathmandu

Place of Gods

Mikel Vause

*...four People's Liberation Army soldiers awaited the expedition,
their pea-green uniform jackets unbuttoned and their cheeks chapped
the color of radiation. They stared
without amusement...—Jeff Long*

Chocolate Himalayas
Sun-burnt plain
Blue water elbows through gravel bars
Mud-brick houses behind skeleton elms
Bony branches cling tattered prayer flags
Like so many rags

Dusty old road to Lhasa
Now gray-black tarmac
Stretches a graceful arch
Cuts through bowels of solid rock
Links past with present

From mind's eye
The isolated and forbidden
City of legend, city of explorers
Treasures legion

A thousands years sacrosanct
Potala Palace explodes heavenward
From Mount Marpori
White-rust walls crowned with gold

Drepung Monastery
Ancient tombs of Lamas
Young monks study ancient text
Sacred silence broken by his cell ring

In Lhasa
Yak butter sacrifices
And prayer scarves
Call to God

Tibet Night

Mary Elizabeth Gillilan

Autumnal tilt

the moon rises over

the treeless plain

Mt. Kailash glows

holy light

raw winds blow

a hawk flies

its wing glows

gone.

How It Goes With Light

Laurel Rust

Midday light in the house
spreads and pools here
and there; on the grey slate
tiles behind the wood stove,
on the white metal cabinet doors
beneath the kitchen sink,
on the floor where the dogs
lie in it. Hour by hour the light
roams this house slowly,
thoroughly. I would like to be
so unhurried, so intimate.

Straw Into Gold

Paulann Petersen

Old wives swear that flax
will bleach to silver-white
if laid in the light of a moon.
So a ship is moved on churning salt
by sails made with goods
borrowed from the sun.

Maybe you've seen her,
the one in a corner, too old
to marry. Day after day
to earn her keep, she pumps pumps
a treadle, spinning the tax
of virgin's wool
due from each house.

A king orders his tablecloth
spun with pale fibers
gathered from crumbled rock.
At banquet his guests watch in thrall
as he flings it stained
into the fire. Then plucks it out
burned clean again.

Bless the bridegroom, bless
his clumsy groomsmen who must
make cloth for the bride's gown.
At night the groom undoes each day's
careless work, then makes it anew.
She is wed in the faultless
weave of his hands.

Petersen, con't.

Locked in a story's ordeal,
what can a maiden do but obey?
She must gather and spin
stinging nettles. Her fingers, palms
swell to a fullness of roses
pricked into bloom.

St. Catherine's body tears apart
on the spokes of a great, spinning wheel.
Faster and faster—slowly it whirls her
out of flesh and bone
into the glowing
thread of her passion.

The first Fate, spindle in hand,
makes an umbilical cord.
The second opens her arms
to give it length.
With silver scissor the third Fate
cuts a newborn loose,
spins her into this world.

Sutra and Syntax

Susan J. Erickson

Recite the sutra of yellow: mango,
forsythia, meadowlark, Van Gogh's bed.

With softest moans, the linen
surrenders to the needle's quick stab.

Reversing the adage, the black-headed
grosbeak obeys *heard not seen*.

She traced the entomology of words:
which ones bite, those that bore, which one sting.

I can't speak Italian, but I'm fluent
in the syntax of *la dolce vita*.

Walk to the Ride

Denise duMaurier

Hampstead, London, England

Watch Mum Nature hang pashmina scarves
from the disk lamps of her autumn shop.
Such blends and colours can't be found in stalls
at Camden Market. Schoolgirls and grannies
peer in all day, to watch her work. It takes
three weeks in a tea-chest, powdered with
incense, to sail them here without a wrinkle.
And five minutes earlier out the door, to stop
and gawp, trudging uphill, past her window.
Ducks, with down and feathers tailor-made
for them, don't stare into shops—they steam
like toy freighters, over ponds on Hampstead
Heath—kicking leaves into whirlpools.
My eyes water from the chill, from patchouli
powder and blending dyes. I will have three
shawls, to disguise my plain black coat,
shelter my shoulders from the rain—and drape
myself Dowager Queen of the Bus, until May.

December Snow

Christine M. Kendall

We've had this time of snow
but especially the light—
the silver crystalline glisten of it
illuminating our days,
which had been up until then
endlessly grey, wet, and sullen.

The transformation welcomed,
even after nightfall when the old orchard
trees: filbert, pear, and apples,
cast sinuous, but strong shadows
across the milk-blue snow.

Where usually there is darkness—
every inch of the yard was visible.

Awakened and out of my bed
in the middle of the night,
I paused at the window struck
by the stillness and lambent light outside—
stood in appreciation until chilled,
fully satiated by snow-bright surroundings.

No Marrow

Shannon Laws

I watch you
Hoping around the twigs
Hanging upside down
From the tiniest sliver of wood

Light and carefree
Yet obviously well fed
Beautiful colors
Lovely song

Be more like the birds
They don't worry, I think
How can I when my bones
Are not filled with air
But of heavy marrow?

Heavy with duty and plans
Weighed down with projects
Slighted by calendar dates
And numbers that don't add up

My human flight drags by
Day to day, no bouncing here
But a determined searching
Looking for morsels to feed the spirit

Think like a bird—
I could be one—
Is it the state of mind that matters
or the transformation?

And when do the two become one?
Mind and matter
Flight and fancy
Living and alive

Laws, con't.

We are cousins little bird
As you hop around the maple
Barren of summer leaves
I watch and learn

My untamed past stirs in the blood
Reminding me of the origins
Forcing breath of life into
The marrow that weighs me down

my cat purrs

through silence

Cottonwood seeds drift

— Andrew Shattuck McBride

The Dream of Love in the Dream of a Heart Transplant

Andrea Carter

The Pacific Northwest's first artificial heart patient to leave the hospital on his own, returns to receive a real heart transplant. September, 2012.

Would it be infidelity? A transplant?
The ultrasounds showed us
arteries like lightning cracks
inside you. Too thin, said the doctor,
the walls closing in—will you too
carry the artificial organ, its motor
in a gray backpack, its clear
vacuum tube running your rhythms,
the orange plastic atria so hard,
culled in the nest of you until—

It comes like a goldfish prize, only
larger, in a white paint container.
Instead of goldfish size, its dimensions,
like a blowfish floating in a zip lock bag,
two yellow eyes look for connective
valves, innocent in ice. In one body
then in another. Is this the test
of love we work toward?

I dream I am the immaculate
surgeon, aluminum picks and forceps;
magnifying lenses provide vision
not just to see which vein goes to which,
but joining tissue to life, kissing the fissures
of valve seams closed. I could master
all the great worlds, all the matter of the universe,
just to feel that beat-beat. That music, infinite.

Carter, con't.

Blood and birth. The applause deafening.
I would say congratulations to you
and your antibodies. But will you still
love me with someone else's heart?

Unlimited Absolutes

Jim Reese

*Get your ass up off the couch
and get a job! We're broke and
I'm pregnant.* A student standing outside my office
screams into her cell phone. *There. You know, now.*

All these broke students with their unlimited plans,
unlimited minutes to text and converse—how I love
your absolutes. No money for infant formula.
No money for lunch;
but there you are hunched over,
fingers moving frantically,
showing the world the top of your head.
I often imagine your lifelines
gone sour—no bars to connect. You stranded
on the shoulder of Highway 81 unable to drive—
pounding your head
against the window.
Now what!
Now what?
I might stop to help. But not today.
Today I'm grading stories about runners.
Everyone is running this semester,
cataloging the city and explaining in great detail
the taint in their pants.
Runners find this humorous.
One essay mentions too many
blueberry lagers before taking off into the
cool moon's gaze.
One finds it necessary to go into great detail
about remnants left on the soles of her shoes.
I lay dying here in your defecations—these woes
that mold you.

Reese, con't.

I wanted to be loved once.
And at the end of the story isn't that what we all ask for?
But, I'm afraid you've violated my mind this time.
Honestly, I don't care about your shit—
really. I don't want to read about it.

First Walks

Janet Oakley

Hazy blue sky. Bunch grass trembling at their seeded heads. There is almost total silence except for the distant rumbling of farm machinery somewhere deep in the Methow Valley below.

A couple walks by.

How many times did we do that? Two-thousand, ten-thousand? How many times in thirty-one years?

I walked with you first on a trail up in the Koolau's, a jungle tangle on the way to Manoa Falls. It smelled of plumeria and over-ripe *lilikoi*, pale, yellow and smooth as chili peppers. The trail was muddy from its daily wash of rain, leaving boot prints and sandals of a score of others.

I didn't know you well then, but I learned to love your back as you went ahead, strong and powerful, your shaggy golden hair rebelling from your tour of duty in a deep jungle far away. Your feet were eager on the trail.

This place where I sit is like the mountains behind Kailua-Kona several months ahead where we scrambled through *a'a* and *pahoihoi* cutting at our boots and the straw brown grasses I cannot name. We found *ohelo* berries sacred to Pele and learned the local joke of 'Oh, Hell' berries. We stuffed them in our pockets and ate them one by one as we sought out *ne ne* and *heiau* and the goat herd hut where we spent the night at 20° above.

I know I loved you then. You were golden, my serendipity.

The sun is hot where I sit. It's turning westward and towards winter, but it still makes sharp shadows on my jeans and on the grass. Too soon, you have passed on before me. My walks with you are over.

You are so far away.

I listen for birds.

You taught me about pheasant, chukker, and turkey and how they hide. You taught me about early morning and shooting stars at the breath of dawn. You taught me to listen, wait, and see. Without you I never would have seen.

High above a jet plane tails across the sky leaving a ghostly white line.

A crow calls.

I miss you.

Choice

James Bertolino

When we make a turning
half-step in our lives
and are taken by an ecstasy

that addles the water
in our cells, that cloaks
the deepest organs in a glow,

we do not lean coolly away
and consider from whence
this enlivening has come.

No, we are in every strand and
striation grateful for this
moment that proves the soul.

We must accept this fondling
of the gods, or ever be
orphans of choice.

At Adrianne's House On Patmos

Joseph Powell

The lemon trees curl inward
and the warmth is a soft net over us,
a cloud so full of itself
it's about to rain, pulsing its blue
shadows across the evening.
The musk of our bodies, the earth
tensing with the thought of rain.

What's knowledge against this?
Or the crude maps of our best intentions?
Our inwardness can be a cathedral
to pleasure's ruin.
Yet the delirium, the blood-hum,
is simple as gravity, diastole & systole.

A cat creeps toward the night.
Moonlight will ignite its eyeteeth
and shine the lemons. A still lizard
watches from a crevice in the whitewashed wall.
We wait for the word, the weight
that will alter the tense balance,
for a lemon to release its purchase,
the lizard to flinch, for the cloudburst.

Everything we love about each other
over these last decades
climbs like the light up this tree,
until the fragrant dark enters us
the way we've entered each other,
and the book sits on its wings,
the cup in its saucer, the shoe's tongue loosened,
and all our sweet undoings are undone.

Wine Dark Sea

Samuel Green

for Paula Meehan

Ah, there it is! Just as you said,
the color of strong Samos wine,
dark as blood on a stone,
not the deep blue of the day, the turquoise
of shallows. Chips of stars, a thin tiara
of moon—as much as might show
in a girl's thick hair. It's what Orestes
must have seen when he raised the temple
up the hill to Artemis, almost believing
a man might drink & drink & still
contrive to make it home.

Sometimes

Judith Azrael

There is a window

in my heart

that is open

Dragonflies dance there

and crickets sing

I play my flute

I brush my hair

Book Review

Michael Daley

The covers of this book are too far apart—Ambrose Bierce

Faces need to be measurable
to mean more than rumpled flesh,
to mean intimacy
within the interruption of our talk.
Your mouth turns down is mystery,
brow lifts, the answer.
A day moth flutter across your lip,
an unrehearsed animal
clean as a lavender petal tipped to the rain.
Below our cliff worn white by Greek sun
she who holds the grand mask witnesses.
The face a hidden poker hand,
the man superior to us covers his mouth
the way a flirtatious stranger does, bus full of eyes,
stage furniture hammered in a dream.
The face before it experiences a self
floats through traffic,
but once asked, the self rides shotgun.
And like roulette, its bullet has our number.
Barnacle by the sea, as yet unfed by tides,
or a conch, one's face weathers the tedium of waves.
Or a novel held too close to the eye;
massive hands slowly press, the covers of a slim book
gently, irrevocably, on far too many pages.

Lovebugs, Part 2

Dayna Patterson

When I remember how you left,
with scorpions in your voice,

off to your big, important job,
I'm reminded of lovebugs,

the thrum of their wings in May,
thoraxes bright red beads on threads of sky.

During mating season, the adult females
only live a few days, the males a little longer,

but not much. A pair lands and creeps awkwardly
across our bedroom window. She seems to drag

his small body where she goes,
and when she decides to fly, his body,

limply obedient, follows.
They might have been us

in reverse.
Goodbye is a knife

I don't throw.

Guitar

Nancy Takacs

I want to pick it up again,
play a little Cat Stevens,
Joni Mitchell, train myself
again to sing in key, capo up,
blood-let against the strain of *Wild Horses*,
ease into *Sunshine on My Shoulders*
with John Denver in the garden,
not looking over my shoulder
to see if my neighbors are listening.

I should just slip it out
of its pillowcase in the fruit room
and let my fingers ride the chords,
G, C, D, G, C, D, FF, GG.
What was that song that took my
pinky a month to callous up?

I used to just pick it up
and play in perfect rhythm,
unleash my loud soprano
for anyone I could get
to listen, take it everywhere with me,
ask for it to be marked
Fragile on planes.

I might only get away now
with a growl like the leads
in *Morbid Angel, Pestilence,
Napalm Death, Dismember,*
or *Pungent Stench,*
some of my son's favorites.
He still plays, but says he lacks
the tremolo for death metal,
his green electric usually cased

Takacs, con't.

under a stack of his Photography II's
abandoned buildings in which he appears
double-exposed like a naked star
born among riffs of rubble.

Sometimes I want Lennon
to play *Imagine* for me on
vinyl, Hendrix to shed his hat
with *Purple Haze,* shed his vulnerable
love of fame, but still pick
strings with his teeth,
light his guitar on fire
and smash it, but not die young.

It surprises me now that most
of my former listeners too are dead,
time humming along when I had them
cornered in an incense-filled living room.

Those old guitarists had
hands like wild anemones.

Some of those I used to love
have voices hard to listen to,
still cranking out albums
I guess because the frets
still call and call them.

Or else they broke
their last string decades ago
and become another self,
never wanting to perform again,
becoming instead
a moon shadow.

An excerpt from: No Guarantees, *a novel-in progress.*

The Wedding

By J. Jamieson Woods

Athin wisp of smoke rose above the treetops that covered the foothills of the Chugach Mountains. In the distance the twinkling lights of Anchorage gave evidence to the spread of the city below. The source of the smoke was the fire in a wood stove that warmed a small cabin nestled in the side of the hill. It was lit up only by the glow of a kerosene lantern. The young couple who lived in this cabin was finishing up their evening meal. Rod, a stocky man in his early twenties, had a full dark beard and piercing brown eyes. Stephanie, still a teenager, was petite and almost waifish with her thin face and anxious light blue eyes. Rod's long, dark hair was thick with a wave that echoed the curl of his beard. Stephanie's hair was also long but thin and straight, the color of dark honey. Both of them had bought into the hippie movement of the '60s, still popular a decade later in Alaska. Stephanie's green tunic was festooned with embroidery and small mirrors that when she moved, reflected the orange glow of the fire in the wood stove. Rod was clad in well worn Levis and a plaid flannel shirt.

The exterior of the humble abode was made from sheets of plywood hammered together to create a basic slant roof cabin, which was a mere 320 square feet. The inside walls bore the foil sheen of the insulation that kept out the deep Alaskan cold. Pink fluff peeked out at the edges of the interior walls. The wood stove served as a cooking source as well as welcome warmth on this chilly April night when the cold hung over the small home. Since they lived many miles out of town there was no need for privacy and the full storey windows gave way to the night outside as well as the view of the lights of the city below.

Stephanie cleaned up after their meal while Rod sat on the love seat, the only furnishing save a wooden ladder back chair. With a beer in one hand Rod watched as his girlfriend poured heated water from the stove into a tub so she could wash the dishes. He stroked his beard and then said, "I guess we should get you some pregnant clothes?"

Stephanie resisted the urge to correct him, *don't' you mean maternity clothes?* But he seemed to be sincere and she didn't want to break the spell of the moment.

Then he followed with, "Maybe my sister has some."

"You are right she probably does. She's about my size don't you think?"

"I think so. Too bad you're not going to stay cute and skinny for much longer, baby. But there's one problem if we ask my sister for her pregnant clothes then she'll put two and two together; she's not stupid. Why in the hell would I be asking her for her pregnant clothes? Of course if she finds that out then she'll tell me to marry you."

"Is that so bad?"

"I told you I don't want to get married."

"I know I heard you." And she returned to her clean-up duties.

A long spell of silence was broken when Rod said, "Oh alright, I'll marry you, just nothing fancy. Let's just go to the courthouse. No big fanfare. We'll tell people afterwards."

Stephanie could feel her relief and excitement but she dared not say anything too telling. "Oh Rod, do you really mean it?"

"Better say, yes, now quick before I change my mind."

"Yes Rod, yes, I will marry you."

"Enough said, don't be blabbing all over let's just go down to the courthouse and get it taken care of and then we can tell people if we want."

The clean-up finished, Rod took the kerosene lantern in one hand and with the other hand, held onto to the rung of the ladder that led up to sleeping loft. Looking into her eyes he said softly, "Come on, baby, let's go have some pregnant sex." She followed him up the ladder. After she was nestled down in bed he lifted the chimney and blew out the lantern with one quick breath. So much for Sunday.

The jeep rumbled along the dirt road to the cabin as they wended their way up the hill to the cabin. They shared some snippets about their Mondays at work. Stephanie had a typical day at the restaurant with the lunch rush just as hectic as usual; Rod said that there was a new shipment of furniture in at the warehouse so he and his forklift had put in a more than a full day. There was a lull in conversation as the jeep rattled on when Rod with one hand on the wheel, the other stroking his beard said, "There is a three day waiting period for a courthouse wedding. Do you want to get married this Friday?"

"This Friday?" Stephanie could hardly believe what she had just heard.

"Yeah this Friday, if you get off by 3, I'll take the afternoon and we can go to the courthouse and get hitched."

This was all happening so fast that Stephanie was having a hard time getting her mind wrapped around the fact that she and Rod were going to get married. This is what she wanted wasn't it?

Marriage is a big deal, Stephanie thought to herself. Rod said he didn't want her to blab to everyone but she wanted to tell her sister. But then when she thought about her mother she felt guilty. She had not yet told her devout Catholic mother that she was pregnant. Her mother would be furious that her daughter had sex outside of marriage. Despite this Stephanie knew that her mother would also be relieved that she and Rod were getting married. Briefly she visited some of the other thoughts that darted in and out of her mind: friends telling her that her life would be essentially over, the waitress with the young son who said that all she did was look after kids and work. There was some truth there. How supportive would Rod be? Would he be the kind of father who changed diapers? Got up at night? How was she going to have a baby in that little cabin way outside of Anchorage? She would be so isolated out there off the maintained roads with no running water or electricity? She really did have a lot on her plate and how was she going to deal with all of it? Well one thing she knew was that she and Rod were getting married on Friday and this was Monday.

After the dinner dishes were done Stephanie sat down next to Rod on the love seat, and took his hand. "What about rings, Rod? Shall we have rings when we get married on Friday?"

"I don't want a ring," Rod said "I work with big equipment, baby. I don't want to get my finger caught on some screw sticking out. Nope no ring for me, baby. But if you want one go ahead and get one."

Stephanie was silent for a bit, and then pulled herself together. "I thought that the guy buys the ring for the girl."

"This is the seventies, women's lib and all that, you want a ring, baby; you buy it yourself."

She tried to hide her hurt and said, "Be that way. I'll get myself a nice one."

After work on Wednesday Stephanie walked from the restaurant to the shopping area of downtown Anchorage. She was looking for a gold ring and a pretty blouse to wear for the wedding. At a store called Raja of India she finally settled on a white gauzy peasant blouse and some patchouli oil to wear for fragrance.

The ring proved to be more difficult to find. She just wanted a simple gold band with maybe a stone, preferably a sapphire on it. She had $50.00 to spend. The quality jewelry stores lowest priced wedding bands started at $300.00. "You know you can always get some nice wedding rings from pawnshops," one kindly woman had mentioned. "People get divorced or die or they just plain need the money so they sell their ring to a pawnshop."

With a cordial good-bye Stephanie headed out in the direction of the pawnshop a few blocks away. She didn't really like the idea of buying a ring that was from a divorce or a death, but she didn't want some cheap ring either, she wanted a real gold ring. *A cheap ring means a cheap marriage,* she thought. *I'm going to do what I can to make this marriage last.*

Hesitantly she entered the shop: the walls were hung with rifles, guitars, banjos, even a violin. There were racks of fur coats and arctic weather clothing. When Stephanie stepped to the counter she felt a bit shy but the guy at the pawn shop knew exactly what she wanted: "A wedding band, yup, I've got lots of them—seems like money is more important to some people than sentiment." He brought out a tray of rings all sizes, some with gems, some without.

Stephanie tried a few on. She found a thin band with a small diamond in it. "How much is this one?" she asked.

"Two-hundred." the man answered.

She slipped the ring off her finger and put it back into the tray. The next few she tried were too big.

"How much you got?" asked the pawnshop man.

"Fifty dollars."

He looked over the rings and picked out a plain thin gold band, "Try this," and he handed it to her.

It was very plain but it fit and looked nice on her hand. "I'll take it," and Stephanie got out her money.

She took off the ring and handed it to the pawnshop man. "You wouldn't happen to have a box for it?"

He leaned down and rummaged under the counter and presented a little white square cardboard box. He handed Stephanie both the ring and the box and said "It's good that you are getting married little lady, I'd say you need someone to look after you and your baby."

Stephanie was quite surprised that he knew she was pregnant. *Oh well,* she thought, *it won't matter, by Friday I'll be married and then it will be OK that I'm pregnant.*

Right on time that Friday, Rod came to get Stephanie from the restaurant. He sauntered in, and said to her, "Are you ready to get hitched, baby?" Stephanie was relieved that there was no one else up front in the restaurant.

She said, "Let me get my coat," and hurried to get the bag that held her new blouse and her wedding ring. After she put the blouse on she daubed some patchouli oil behind her ears, on her wrists and between her breasts. She brushed her hair and checked herself out in the mirror. She thought she looked pretty good with her white blouse and dangly pearl earrings. She then put her coat on overtop. The groom isn't supposed to see the bride before the wedding. She felt like a little kid getting away with wearing her church dress to school.

At the courthouse there was a couple ahead of them who were just coming out. The bride wore a gauzy dress, and the groom, a plaid flannel shirt much like Rod's. *The couple sort of resembles Rod and me*, Stephanie thought, *except the new bride didn't look pregnant.* They were holding hands and kissing as they walked. They were obviously happy to be married.

Rod and Stephanie sat on the bench outside the courtroom. "Well the last time I here was three years ago."

"What!" Stephanie tried not to screech. What was he doing here three years ago?

"Yeah, baby, I guess I didn't tell you I got busted for pot three years ago. It's not that big a deal here in Alaska."

"But you got busted….by the police?"

"Yeah, who else busts you? It's not a big deal," he said again "It's just a misdemeanor in Alaska. No biggie."

"Why didn't you tell me?"

"Why didn't you ask me?"

"Why didn't I ask you, why would I ask you?

Just then the court reporter came out "Kolber, wedding are you ready?"

Rod stood up, relieved to get out of the conversation about him getting busted.

Stephanie removed her coat revealing her new blouse and perhaps the scent of her patchouli. If Rod noticed he did not offer any comment.

The ceremony was over in a few minutes. Stephanie forgot to give Rod the ring, so when the judge asked if they had rings Rod said, no, and she said, yes, at the same time. She then retrieved the box out of her pocket and gave it to him.

"Thanks," he opened the box and tried the ring on his own finger "Too small, baby, looks like you planned on marrying a much smaller guy."

"No that ring is for me, you said you didn't want a ring, remember?"

"That's right. Here, baby," he chortled as he slipped the ring onto her finger.

"I now pronounce you man and wife," said the judge.

They were now officially married. Rod gave her a kiss and said, "Come on baby let's go get drunk."

Lethe's Poppy

Paulann Petersen

I am the consolation begun
before dust, before even the black
drift of seed. An ease
reaching down with white roots.
My embrace surrounds
the blinded stone, every
fat-meated corm.
Far, yes, under the ground,
my swollen nodes
grip clay and shifted silt.

Stories predict red,
silk crinkles fine enough
to be made and erased
by a smile. So be it.
I do bloom, and leave
a temple-pod crowned
by a circle of high, shaded
windows. Look into them,
Look out. Beneath lies
a belly swollen with seed
fine as dust—endless
bewitchment, the mending
husk of sleep.

Guilty

Nancy Takacs

First the fire
in the dry gray hills.
Then ashes like a dust devil
in the lavender night sky.

You blossom with needlepoint,
are sewn full with melon peonies,
clap one hand against the envelope of fear.

You dragonfly swollen rivers
in your turquoise dizziness,
eyes of jet-lag,
wings of crinoline.

Small red letters glow
and fade under your breast,
as you sleep:
Black Dragon Canyon,
steep patina walls,
spiderweb of trails.

You're now a lifelong member
of *Natural History.*

You're an invasive tamarisk
leaning over a drawer of whitewater.

~

Guilty rides in on a dirt-bike,
her blonde hair below a helmet
airbrushed with a tiger pounce,
her legs in white leather,
shoulder tattooed in a sunrise
over children's names,

Takacs, con't.

women's reaching hands,
her arm thick with roses
of unanswered emergencies.

The dry wash she upsets
with her bludgeoning tires
blooms with jitters
of sego lilies, blue mustard,
turns to a seeping spring
with hanging gardens.

Such a hot day, and the shade
has disappeared, but
she holds out her hands
under the iron-colored
water, and breathes.

Four Questions And

Rosemerry Wahtola Trommer

are you sharing it
with me, this
loneliness?

*

how do they do it,
those birds, keeping a course
through the gale
when even in this still, still room
I can hardly take one step

*

alone is more
alone than
I thought

*

as I fall
I feel how this, too,
is dancing

*

that small voice,
quiet as petals, says
why not be the one
who tears down any wall
that stands between two hearts

*

Wahtola Trommer, con't.

falling, falling,
I don't know when I stopped
wanting to be caught

*

new snow in the field
the only tracks there
one woman dancing

*

they sure do mess up
the sheets—excitement
and grief

*

who is the one
that falls and who is the one
who notices her falling

*

midnight
the power out, I make
of myself a light

In the Long Shadow of the Wasatch
Mikel Vause

Long rows of mud lark nests
Like inverted volcanoes
Chocolate brown, wild with dry grass blades
And yellow wheat straw
Cling to rust-colored steel girders

Of a government building
Every few seconds
Black feathered orange beaked rockets
Explode as from the earth's core
Blurs of black, yellow, and red streak the azure sky
Rip through wispy clouds
Hang like prayer flags strung from Ben Lomond's summit

Mud larks bank sharply drop and dart through flagging
Cat Tails and Bull Rushes
Insects hover over murky motionless water of Bear River
A trickle in the high Unitas
Cuts a sacred and circuitous path
Through alpine forests
Orchards and farm lands
For 500 miles to the salt marshes of Great Salt Lake

Snowy Egrets stand like statues
On spindly legs
In search of fish and frogs
Mosquitoes and midges
And pull with needle sharp beaks
At tender green tubers from the murky water

Great Blue Herons and
Pelicans feed on sluggish carp
And channel cats
All the while squadrons

Vause, con't.

Of Canada Geese pass in formation overhead
Toward breeding grounds in the Arctic

Bald Eagles, Nature's spy planes
Launch out from hidden bases in the western Wellsvilles
Circle over slow-moving water and frosted alkali flats
Then drop like a bolt
And with black razor talons
Carry off carp, channel cat, or cotton tail

This is a place of spirit
God's hand clearly present
Brings together
Burrowing Owls, Avocets, Swans
Ducks, Grebes, Northern Harriers
Long Billed Curlew, Peregrine Falcons
White Faced Ibis, muskrat, fox, deer,
Skunk, rabbit, field mouse, water snakes

This place of sorrowing stillness,
Of perfect symbiosis
Life cycles endless and never failing
"Survival here is earned never granted."

Ancestor

Peggy Shumaker

There, claws sunk in a river snag,
hangs a wrinkly skinned

iguana as long as I am tall.
I can't explain his goiter, nor

the prickles beneath his chin.
Along his back vestigial spines

droop like a bad comb-over.
One eye he keeps on us

while we steal closer.
Why hang there in the heat,

instead of bellying up
to the mudbank?

Maybe to him, one
who must take in

whatever warmth
he's going to have,

this choking sauna's
as close to nirvana

as this incarnation's
going to get.

The Pass Over

Joseph Powell

A flock of sunlit swans
flies down our winter river.
The new snow spread like a clean tablecloth—
so cold the ice-flecked air diamonds.
An arresting rarity in this valley
they unzip the day and divide
silence from the need for silence.

Discussing our failed allegiances
we stopped our walking
to let the image of what we almost ruined
pass over us like a squad of angels
who worked all night
going from doorpost to doorpost
but finding no one to blame.

Carrying the morning on their backs,
they're returning to a lake
that can still hold their reflections,
like a thought its glimmer of feeling.
When they finally disappear
into the path of their journey
like lit water poured into a body of water
we feel rinsed, ready to go on.
How quiet the morning becomes.

Girl, Gathering

Laurel Rust

This morning the night's snow
was a thin white cloth
that held us all.
By afternoon it had unraveled
and we were each
only ourselves again: green
spikes of daffodils,
saturated ground,
winter branches, a girl
gathering what she could and
pressing it
with reddened hands
into a ball.

Gooseberry

Samuel Green

At night, when we sleep,
something eats the leaves
of the gooseberry, leaves them
ragged, like the edges of pages
torn from a church hymnal.
It is some hidden worm, we guess,
but the soil at its base
yields nothing, nothing shows
in the glare of the flashlight after dark.
Each day the green edges recede,
until only the ridiculous thorns
are left threatening the air.
We try diatomaceous earth, tanglefoot,
powders & sprays, remove the fallen
leaves & re-till the ground around
the trunk. Carbolic acid doesn't work,
nor foxglove infusions, nor offhanded
prayer. What we know is something
needs a care we cannot measure
up to. Something else works in the dark,
more patient, more hungry, more sure.

Daylight

Sara E. Simard

Purple horizon.
Peach-colored lake.
Douglas Fir trees
a royal forest green

Stellar Jays strike
at panes of glass.
Other wild birds
rip and tear.

A lone feeder found.
Homemade suet
gone. Seeds fallen
out of sight.

Sumas Mountain Meditation

James Bertolino

The distance within
certain people's minds between
the firm seat of rationality
and far landscapes of fantasy

can be exhilarating to float, or fly.
The ultimate descent can, of course,
be precipitous, can bring disorientation
and pain. But don't flights

into the unknown always generate risk?
And can vital verses ever be born
to those whose life-patterns
are risk-averse?

The Royal Hudson
Christine M. Kendall

At the window of Fairhaven Library
looking towards Bellingham Bay I saw her
round Post Point, a plume of white smoke
making a 45 degree bend above her stack,
jet black engine gleaming in sunlight.

Momentarily, the sighting felt normal
as if witnessed on a daily basis
despite my being mesmerized by it,
then, I realized—I lived in another era—
in another time.

Hadn't I read somewhere the steam train
Royal Hudson made a special trip to Seattle
and now was returning home to Canada?

Yet, I've often wondered about
the moment I saw her
how she felt so familiar,
so much a part of my life—
had she been one day,
one life before?

A New Sound

Rosalyn Ostler

*Sing unto the Lord, all the earth...Let the sea roar
...let the fields rejoice...Then shall the trees of the wood sing out
at the presence of the Lord...* I Chronicles 16

Imagine sounds of earth in singing;
the metal voice of vibrant rocks,
a steady tuning fork now ringing

as rich and deep as tones of Bach's
grand fugues, with counterpoint from notes
of breathy song by pine and hemlocks.

Now listen to the crooning throats
of wind. Orchestral forests strum
woodsongs, diverse as leaves, that float

to blend and rise with earth's rich hum.
The sound intensifies and fills
with praise the air that once was dumb.

A maple song created, spilled,
the baritone of sycamore,
the rippling aspen's high-pitched trill,

join other tongues and sound a chord,
a strain of worship through the trees.
All sway to hymns that wreathe and soar

to blend with rhythm from the seas.
The chanting waves curl edges, white
as joy, against sand's harmonies.

Ostler, con't.

The glow of rising morning light
chimes pink from heaven's throne,
joins tinkling stars in chorus, bright

harmonic sun, moon's mellow tones.
Sky's choir combines with woven song
below of reverent stream and stone.

The psalms of daisies, lupine throng
with hummingbirds' and eagles' phrases,
the crickets' patterned evensong,

the bugling moose, as earth obeys its
earnest need: sing praises, sing praises.

Tree Reflections

Betty Scott

Winter tree,
your shadow
is a blackened
crucifix,

your morning
wind dance,
a silent
swaying.

Christmas hologram,
your leafless
limbs are
wise men

bearing gifts
of despair
joy and mystery,
your branches

upturned.
I recall
beloved arms
of a sleeping baby.

Bellingham Coal Train

Allen Frost

I hear the cry
deep at night
after 3 A.M.
when I can't sleep
they roll that coal
in open car
after car
right through town
to haul it away
to China

It must be the debt
for all our war
to have to dig
out our heart

How else could we
collapse so far
every bullet, every filthy
hand greased
from here to there

That sound
brings up questions
how much is left
how much more
can be hollowed out
where is it from
how far do the tracks go
who are we fooling
these trains
tugging at
black veins

Frost, con't.

Vampires
running dark at night
people will stop
drop their lives
to watch it
rumble through
their neighborhoods
until it's gone
an eerie quiet
left after thunder

I've heard
people who live
close to the tracks
even with windows
closed tight
they still find
soot on the sills
on the cloth curtains
on their furniture
coal dust in the air

We must be
deep in debt
I'm afraid
we must be
miles in the red
digging down
in pockets
finding no more
spare change
coming up with coal

Two Views Of The Wreckage
John Morgan

[Note: Climate change models show interior Alaska becoming dryer while coastal areas flood worldwide]

Kibitzing over your shoulder as you
sketch those billowing clouds above the
staved-in houseboat in its dried up slough,
I sense the berrying bear that ambled by a
day or two ago leaving this gritty substance,
fear, like a pheromone, hanging there
and there—and because we codgers share
a wish to buck the laws of change and chance

you cache the present scene while I flash on
distant glittering Venice seen back when
the band played gaudy Liszt and Beethoven
and Sputnik shimmered over St. Mark's Square
where now high waters climb the palace stair
as ice-sheets thaw and toxic tides roll in.

for the artist, Kes Woodward

Arrival

Luther Allen

we are watched over

by rocks, kept

waiting, hoping

in quest of

just one sunrise

that might

for even a second

wake us, them

Greenways

Stephanie Cosky Hopkinson

The forest is skinned of trees
its flesh sliced apart in truck-sized lengths
limbs piled high and left to rot

New houses blister the land,
3-bed 2-bath tumors fed by pipes
buried alongside the forest's broken bones

Now just a thin green buffer of trees and brush
winds along the twisting creek, fitted with a wide path and safety handrails
so I can walk easy under shimmering leaves

I try. But the birds keep screaming over a limp hamburger wrapper
and the beaten down banks of the sterile creek smell of waste.
There are trees, but I can't pretend I'm walking in the forest

Because what I'm really doing
is crawling like a hungry beetle
along the last stringy scraps of a corpse

Scar

Jon D. Lee

Come down fast from a forest of scrub oak into a wide meadow tinged bloody by a full moon shining through flat heat-fumed horizon, car wheels spinning fast so old suspension can't push back into half-overgrown twin dirt ruts, car seeming to float above earth but for the off-timed thud of rear wheel against wheel well and a half-second later echo from the trunk.

"I hear he done the same thing in Westville," says the driver, tall, head scraping the ceiling.

"Who told you that?" says the man in the middle, this one short, straining to see over the dashboard.

"Thompson," says the driver. "Says he heard it from his cousin who lives over there. Says they run him out of town afterward."

"Don't surprise me," says the third man in the front seat, blond hair moving against the open window. "Once you do it, you're gonna do it again."

"Unless someone stops you," says the driver. "And that's what we're gonna do tonight, ain't it, Timmy?" This last to the rear seat's sole occupant, a mound of flesh spilling over carefully buckled seatbelt.

"Yuh," says Timmy.

"I don't think we should use names," says the short man. "Seems wrong."

"Who you think's gonna hear us?" says the blond man. "'Sides, it ain't like anyone who knows Timmy ain't gonna recognize him from a quarter mile off. Ain't that right, Timmy?"

"Yuh."

"Anyway," says the driver, "whether he done it in Westville or not, he ain't gonna do it again. That's what's important."

Outside the windows red, white, blue wildflowers stained black by shadow slap against chipped paint, rusted muffler.

"If he did do it in Westville," says the blond man, "how'd he get away with it?"

"What?" says the driver.

"How'd he get away with it?" says the blond man.

"I don't know," says the driver. "Probably in a car, I guess. Or bought a bus ticket."

"Could've used the train," offers the short man. "Not a boat, though. No rivers near Westville."

Blond man rolls his eyes. "Not what I meant. I mean, if it was my wife, I'd have him dead before he hit city limits. So how come he's still alive?"

"Oh," says the driver. "Never thought about that. Maybe they give him a good whipping before they run him out. Maybe that was good enough."

"Wouldn't be good enough for me," says the short man.

"Me neither," says the blond man.

"Maybe," says the driver, "they tried to get him, but he got away first."

"Yeah," says the short man. "Like maybe they come after him, but he heard about it, and took off. Or maybe they took a couple shots at him, but missed."

"Wouldn't matter, if it was my wife," says the blond man. "I'd still hunt him down. Wouldn't matter where he went or how long it took. Something like that…well, you don't let people get away with that. What about you, Timmy? You kill him, or just run him off?"

"Yuh."

"That's what I thought."

"Don't use names!" says the short man. "Ain't right."

"Either way," says the driver, "he ain't doin' it again."

"Yuh."

Wildflower, scrub oak, black sky and heat. Full moon crawls a fingernail further, makes shadows shift and slink and writhe on the ground like living things searching for holes in which to bury themselves. Twin dirt tracks veer suddenly left, for a moment the car floats sideways, straightens out.

"Ever wonder why he lives by himself?" asks the blond man.

"What the hell's that got to do with anything?" says the driver.

"Seems strange," says the blond man, shrugs. "He's lived here at least twenty years I know of, and in all that time he's lived alone in that little shack. Come to think of it, I never even heard of him so much as talkin' to a woman before, much less touchin' one, and now this. Seems awful peculiar."

The driver's voice loud, sharp, his eyes slits. "You callin' Miss Jenny a liar?"

"Yuh."

"Shut it, Timmy," says the blond man, without anger.

"Don't use names!"

"Ain't callin' Miss Jenny nothing," the blond man continues. "Just think it's strange it happened now. Maybe he's been on the run too long from them Westville folks. Must've drove himself crazy out there by himself all those years, till finally.... Hell, how'd you feel without a woman that long?"

Red lights flare cinder-bright, are caught up, overtaken by dust clouds, making indistinct the double thump, groan from the trunk.

"What the hell is that got to do with it?" asks the driver, jaw tight.

"Probably nothing," says the blond man, shrugs.

"Damn right, nothing. Now look, he done it, and that's that. We settled?"

"Yuh."

"Shut it, Timmy," says the blond man, then, "Never said we weren't. Just wondered who he is."

"Well don't," says the driver.

Horizon lurches, picks up speed. Smell of oil, dust, old dashboard. Black tree limbs scratch ribbons of moonlight, clutter the border between earth and sky.

"How much longer is it?" asks the short man.

"Not long," says the driver. "Just over that rise."

"You remembered rope, right?"

"'Course I remembered the damn rope. The hell kind of stupid question's that?"

"Just makin' sure," says the short man. "I don't want no surprises."

The car eases up, down the rise, the ground coming in on either side, pinching into a flat peninsula sticking out into a horseshoe bend of a dry riverbed clogged with husks of scrub brush. Dirt tracks split the land in two, lead to the base of a cottonwood long dead and leaning heavily over a crumbling rim.

"That don't look good," says the short man.

"What?" asks the driver.

"That," he says, and points at the tree. "You sure that's gonna hold?"

"It's where they did Jim," says the driver. "It'll hold."

"Yeah," says the blond man. "But that was twenty years ago."

"So?"

"That tree might of been dead longer than you been alive," says the blond man.

"It's where they did Jim," repeats the driver. "It'll hold."

Red lights flare again, then the click-clunk of three doors opening and closing, and four men stand staring at the trunk lid. "Here," says one, and passes around a bottle, and three of them tip it back long, cough briefly.

"We sure about this?" says the blond man.

"Too late now," says the driver, stretching tall. "Gotta be done. Might as well get it over with quick."

A flash of keys and the lid bounces open. The man inside is a thin and shivering lump: wide white eyes, bloody t-shirt, grease-stained jeans, silver duct tape over his mouth and binding his black hands and bare black feet. Shaking fingers spasm around a tire iron he jabs too slowly at the nearest face, swings wildly at the next, then missing that too, holds tightly against his ribcage. A white arm darts in quickly, wrenches the tool away, brings it back to thud dully against the man's side. A grunt of pain.

"Thought you'd've learned your lesson the first time," says the driver. He reaches in, grabs ankles with both hands. "Timmy, you get under his arms."

"Yuh."

Lifted free of the trunk the man thrashes, manages to pull his feet out of the driver's hands, then screams in muffled call as his heels bounce off the dirt tracks.

"Shit," says the driver, squatting to retrieve his load. He jerks his head at the blond man. "Get the middle."

The blond man hesitates, places his arms under the grease-stained jeans and lifts. He sniffs, turns his head. "He pissed his pants."

"You get the rope," the driver says to the short man, then to the blond man, "And don't you let go."

"I won't," is the reply, and four men walk through twin headlight beams, three of them holding a fifth man in a double "H" that wavers like a snake through brown grass, stopping on the near side of the cottonwood tree.

"Alright, just drop him," says the driver. The body thumps down, bony back ricochets off an exposed tree root. Another stifled scream floats into the air, is lost in high branches. "Timmy, you make sure he doesn't go anywhere."

"Yuh."

The short man wrings his fingers around the clutched rope, yellow nylon fibers stretching, groaning. "I really don't think we should be using names," he says, his knuckles white and forehead shiny in the highbeams.

"Shut up, Jerry," says the tall man. "Tie a goddamn noose in that thing. Make yourself useful."

"Don't use my name!" yells the short man. He stares at his hands. "I don't know how to tie a noose."

"Oh, for Christ's sake. You do it then," he says to the blond man.

"I don't know either. And I'm pretty sure Timmy doesn't. Do you?"

"Goddammit!" shouts the driver. "Just tie a couple slipknots in it then. And make sure they're good ones. You know how to do that, right?"

"Of course I do," says the small man, still wringing the yellow fibers. "Why do I have to do it, though?"

"'Cause you're the one holding the goddamn rope!"

"Here, I'll do it," says the blond man, grabbing one end. "Like you said, let's make this quick. I don't want to have to do this twice if the knot doesn't hold." He twists the rope around itself, feeds the loose end through the pretzel hole, repeats the knot several times more, slips the noose around his foot and stands on it, pulls, watches the hole shrink around his shoe. "There," he says.

The small man's forehead wrinkles. "Aren't we supposed to have a chair or something?"

"What for?" says the driver.

"You know, you stand him on it and kick it out from under him."

"Do you see a chair around here?"

"...No," his eyes glancing back toward the car.

"Then that's not how we're gonna do it," finishes the driver. "Just throw the rope over that branch and we'll pull him up by hand."

More stifled screams from the man on the ground. His legs kick against the exposed roots, hands scrabble in the dirt. He manages to get to his knees, is kicked in the chest, falls back hard.

"Everyone clear on the plan?" asks the driver. He grabs the rope before anyone answers, slips the loop over short-cropped curly black hair, wipes his hands on his pants. On the ground the man's eyes are wide, his jaw moving soundlessly against silver tape. "Timmy, stand him up."

"Yuh."

The man stands, shaking, his knees collapse beneath him, hands work the front of his shirt in knotted balls. Snot drips from his nose. He is stood up again, held there easily by Timmy's bulk. The driver throws the rope over a branch, grasps the loose cord several feet from the end, holds the rest out to grab.

"Wait," he says, and smiles, though his eyes don't. "Let's see if there's any last words. What about it? You wanna beg?"

He rips the silver tape away, the skin beneath following, dry lips cracking. A flash of teeth, white against black, snarling, opening, closing.

"Shit!" yells the driver, jerking his hand away, "He bit me!" On the pad of his thumb a double crescent, spots of blood already rising, bursting, running. "Sonofabitch bit me!" He stoops, feels, his hand closes around a rock, smashes it against the man's mouth, the man now mewling, red lips blossoming as he chokes, coughs, white chips hitting the ground in a glob of blood and snot. "Hoist him up!" yells the driver. The air fills with a high-pitched scream, a thick and bubbling "No! No! No! Norrrkkk" the rope stretches tight as silver taped hands grasp at the neck, claw red lines in black flesh. "Pull, goddammit!" yells the driver and three men grunt against the strain, then "Timmy, get over here and help!" the giant bulk standing, mouth open, staring at the man's feet rising, toes just touching the ground, carving notches in the dust, swinging free and jerking, kicking, hands scrabbling against yellow nylon now red and hot and slippery and a pinch of flesh caught in the knot pulls free and a line of broken teeth grinding and now a wet ripping sound and the feet hitting the earth hard, then the knees, the man falls onto his face, coughing, coughing, spitting, coughing.

The blond man rises from where he too fell, eyebrows drawn together, grabs a frayed yellow end and holds it up against the car lights, feels the ripped fibers. "Shit, Frank," he says. "Your rope's rotten."

"What?"

"I said your rope's rotten. This ain't gonna work. Unless you got another piece of rope in there."

The small man breathes shallow, fast, chest shaking. "Jesus Christ!" he yells, his voice high, cracking. "What are we supposed to do now? We can't just leave him here! What the hell are we gonna do?"

"Shut up, Jerry," says the driver. "Lemme think."

"Don't use my name! Don't use my name!" the voice even higher.

The driver moves quickly, grabs the small man by the back of his head, hair clenched in fist, pulls the head back so the face is looking at him with wide eyes. "I swear to Christ," he says, "if you say that one more time I'm leaving you out here too. Now both of you shut up and lemme think." He stands, fists flexing, stares at the man on the ground still coughing, says, "I got an idea."

The blond man moves only his eyes, mouth, "Alright, let's hear it."

"I say we show him what it's like to do what he done to Miss Jenny."

"The hell's that supposed to mean?" says the small man, eyes darting.

"You just leave that part up to me," says the driver. "Paul, go get me that tire iron from the trunk. Timmy…"

"Yuh," still standing, staring, mouth open.

"…you pick him up and hold him again…"

"Yuh."

"...and Jerry, you come over here."

"Why? What do you want me to do?"

The driver's lip curls, his hands flex. "I want you to take his pants off."

"What?" says the small man, not moving. "The hell you wanna do that for?"

"I told you," is the slow reply. "I'm gonna show him what it's like to do what he done to Miss Jenny."

The blond man now back, hands the tire iron off, glances at the driver through slits. "I don't want no part of no queer sex."

"Ain't gonna be no queer sex," says the driver. "That's what the iron's for. You got him, Timmy?"

"Yuh."

"Bend him over."

A high groan, white eyes flicker open, peer through black lids. "Pleashh," the man says, his lips and tongue thick and bloody, the words slurred and bubbling, "No, pleashh."

"Bend him over, Timmy. That's right, just like that," says the driver.

"Pleashh…"

"Now Jerry, you get his pants off…"

"Pleashh," a weak struggle, but the body is held firm.

"…Paul, you might need to help hold him."

"Pleashh…"

"What the hell are you gonna do, Frank?" says the blond man.

"Just you leave that to me."

"Pleashh…"

"Jerry, get those pants down around his ankles."

"I don't think I want to, Frank."

"Pleashh…"

"Goddammit Jerry, don't make me use this on you," the tire iron held high, gray metal against black sky. "Don't forget you're part of this too. Now get those goddamn pants off!"

"Pleashh!" said louder, and again, quickly, "pleashh!"

"Somebody shut him up!" yells the driver.

"Can't, Frank," says the blond man. "There's no more tape."

"Pleashh!" struggling now, small frame squirming.

"Jerry, hurry up!"

"Frank…"

"Goddammit Jerry," tire iron drawn back, arm flexed, "Do it!"

"No! Pleashh!"

Trembling hands move forward, around ("Pleashh!"), unfastening, struggle with the zipper ("No! Pleashh!"), the man bucking hard now but held fast, blond man stepping forward and grabbing an arm ("Pleashh No! Pleashh!"), black feet moving farther apart to keep the pants in place, kicked roughly back ("Pleashh!"), the small man now grabbing belt loops and yanking, yanking ("Pleashh!"), squatting to pull harder, face red and wet, then pausing, staring at empty spaces ("Pleashh…"), dropping the belt loops and falling backwards, landing in dirt and blood and broken teeth. "Jesus Christ!"

The driver's brows knit together, "What the hell are you doing, Jerry?"

"Jesus Christ!" crawling backward in the dirt, his eyes wide, "Jesus Christ!"

"What the hell's gotten into you?" snarled through gritted jaw.

"Jesus Christ, there's nothing there!"

"Nothing where?"

"Jesus Christ, Jesus Christ, there's nothing there! Jesus Christ!" The small man now standing, turns, runs past the car and into the darkness, "Jesus Christ! Jesus Christ!" fading into the open air, hot and still.

"The hell was that about?" says the driver. "Goddamn Jerry losing it at a time like this, I'm gonna kick his ass when we get back to town. You two, stand him up and turn him around, let's just beat the shit out of him and go." The tire iron raised again, pulses, then lowers, pauses, slips though loose fingers as the driver stares at the figure before him, his eyes searching, darting from knee to stomach to knee to stomach. "Holy shit," he says quietly, and the tire iron clunks dully against the ground, "Holy shit." He swallows, blinks, Timmy and the blond man staring at him, each other, "Holy shit," he says again, and then, "Let's just go. Let's just go. Let's just go."

The blond man frowns, begins to speak, looks down at the man and then his hands fall away too, slap against his legs. "Holy shit," he agrees, backs away, cuts through a headlight beam that winks against the tree. "Timmy, let him go."

"Yuh?"

"Just let him go, Timmy," says the blond man, now at the car door, pulling at the handle, "Just let him go."

The man falls to the ground, is momentarily shadowed, then lit again. Three car doors click open, clunk close. Another click, engine rev, and the lights recede, swing around, become two red lights growing smaller and smaller, while high above the moon glows white and full, shining on the car as it stops, click-clunk, starts again, shining on dust clouds floating though brown grass, shining on the cottonwood tree leaning heavily over the edge, shining on the red blood and the yellow rope and the gray metal tire iron, shining on the man as he curls wetly and darkly around himself on this dry peninsula jutting out into the curl of a dry riverbed, shining on this scar of earth.

Art Appreciation

Andrea Carter

The wood panels closed,
dark and foreboding, as if
to enter a church, a cave, a mouth,
a skull. But opened to expose

The Garden of Earthly Delights
framed between heaven and hell
tiny, fearless, intricate as bugs,
they stand in flower nectaries,

pure and pink, and also letch
behind an acorn hull to attack,
molest, terrorize. How can all this
be in clear lime green, tiger lily hues?

Apple tree roots finger the grass;
ants trail where they must. But are these
humans too? Stealing, drinking, slothing,
and peeing to their hearts' content

Troubled Colloquy

James Bertolino

When the boulder of her grief finally cracked,
it was full of insects.

His internship included doing pastel drawings
of bloodstains in the White House.

She wondered why the priests were wearing
gloves and safety glasses.

If we recognize the war is between demons,
do we care who wins?

Feels So Good to Be So Fat

Jim Reese

I'm increasing my total strides
on the elliptical machine at the wellness and
fitness center, feeling adequate next to the large
man moving ever so slowly and uneasily
on the stationary bike next to me.
And I am in control
of the remote for once, watching
Man vs. Food.

Is this show really necessary? The large man barks.
Give me that remote.

I turn up the volume,
reassure him that it is necessary,
that if the host can consume
the Italian Challenge—seven pounds of chicken parmesan,
Italian sausage, lasagna, spaghetti and meatballs, manicotti,
a whole loaf of garlic bread, fresh salad, cannelloni,
a cup of Italian wedding soup, and an apple crisp dessert
in under 90 minutes,
he wins a t-shirt.

Only been done two times, I add, *ever.*
Increasing my resistance,
I watch my   smart rate
                heart rate
                    peak high.

Can You See Her Fly

Nancy Canyon

Sister cut cardboard wings
to tie with white string over tiny scapulas.

Soon, she'll fly out the attic window,
soar on air currents over the neighborhood.

Mother doesn't hear him creeping upstairs
into her sleeping daughter's room.

While his fingers stray beneath summer covers,
Sister ascends through mottled sunlight,

flying above pines, a tiny angel circling our house,
a secret shoved deep into her PJ pocket.

The Wall

Simon Perchik

This wall is for the map, the rest
to separate the distances
as if they had a beginning, would forget

someone didn't write it down
the way the calendar, by heart
will reach around what happens after

and still recognize a simple shoreline
hidden between the unused years
that no longer protect you

though you let them hold on
as if places mattered
—a single wall, the nail

even when bleeding from its mouth
points out where you are
the rivers and the others.

The Origins of Geography

Gailmarie Pahmeier

In 1966, my father bought a brand new
Pontiac Tempest with a cam engine,
the most beautiful thing I'd ever seen,
champagne colored, thick protective plastic
to preserve the luscious leather seats.
I was proud of that car, its sheer
American bulk and excess.
That was the year we drove to California,
my pink autograph book waiting for stars.
We drove all day, all night, my mother sharing
the wheel, candy and grilled cheese
at truck stops, the sheer joy of going far.
I remember the Grand Canyon, how I told
my sisters one day I'd live there, how I put
a good dent in my savings to buy costume
turquoise, a feather for my hair. In Las Vegas,
my father gambled while my mother walked
with us along Fremont Street, windows
full of glitter and sass. I bought her a black
cigarette holder, six inches of the truest
elegance I'd ever seen, loved watching
her long fingers twirl it as she puffed.

Then Disneyland and the promise of pleasure--
I loved most the talking Lincoln and the Tiki Room,
this beginning of a life of umbrella drinks
and the men who brought them, some as tall
and talkative as Mr. Lincoln himself,
but all of them eager to spend time, money
in places of mercy and darkness.
We'd saved so much for amusement, we dressed
to show it—girls in their summer dresses,
white leather shoes, bows and beads, beautiful
and worthy, our mother with her snap handbag

full of gum and crackers, our father's
pressed slacks. But one sister's shoes cut
into her feet, their crisscross ribbons dug
deeply enough to scar. The baby returned
from the restroom trailing toilet paper
under her ruffles, cried hard, harder
when we laughed, when a man said, *Hey there
where are you girls from? Who dresses up
for Disneyland? What's your origin?*

I didn't know what that word suggested,
had not yet learned to think of birthplace
as stamp. Driving east again that very night,
I slept nearly to Winslow, woke in love
with the car again, my father's tanned arm
resting outside the window, the smell
of Wrigley's gum sweet and utterly
familiar. I had a story to tell everyone
in Joplin, gifts of ashtrays, shrunken heads,
a rabbit fur purse. I told everyone
I'd been out West. I told nobody
its geography of magic and shame.

Delivery

Mary Elizabeth Gillilan

Matthew 5:15

Inside my canvas bag
strapped across my right shoulder
in tissue packed tight, gifts

A street fair—marriage in Lahore
the bride locked in a tiny box
borne by jubilant family men
she handed over
father to father
her wild eyes visible
through painted bars
rock of ages hear me now
rock of ages
hear her, ever?

Grandmother's index finger
white smooth fairy skin
she points to a star
in the Ellensburg Canyon night
rockets with stars
wish and I do

That Parisian elevator boy
bonjour bon soir
lift of glass
eyes liquid blue
broken glass maybe
but I was fourteen

A missal open in my hand

Gillilan, con't.

On a rock that juts
into a swirling sea
I count waves and wait 'til
seven—my store of gifts
await retrieval await
arrival
await

Giving Voice

Anita K. Boyle

Let my voice run along
the wires that bind the earth together.
I believe each of us
should be remembered for our mouths
shaped like our planet:
round, evolving, and in use.

As the first phrase begins, the voice
meets the blink of an owl's eye,
the head turning away,
the confusion at dawn:
an inkling.

I want to understand the choir
that moves like rocks down the river;
or like the eerie yipping of the pack
at night; or the combined howling
of poets, those fine threads
twined together syllable by syllable.

My voice is a burst
of cottonwood fluff floating
on a spring breeze, littering
the paths in the park. What's the difference
if the world is one voice richer
or poorer?

The tongue picks letters
from the throat, places them as words
on the palate, counts the spacing
between the teeth,
and prints them on the wind.
Do not pick them up until the ink dries;
they'll smudge, become illegible.

Boyle, con't.

The hatchling's yellow-rimmed beak
rises just above the mud-
lined circle of nest as it
chirps its first to the sun.
The reward: a mouthful of worms.
I want to open my voice
and get that earthy taste
of satisfaction.
I want to open my mouth
and have it mean something.
Anything.

Fragment of poem written by Nelle McLeod Anderson Brown Johansen (1896-1966) in Fishtown on the Skagit River and note written on backside of it.

The Fragment

You start to fish as day is done
and don't pick up 'till rising sun
If fish keep coming all the season
a stake I'll make or know the reason.

The Note

Some guys up at La Conner say Clarence didn't catch those 37 Tyees but got them from non-union fisherman. It's a <u>damn</u> lie as I saw him catch them all. <u>Sour Grapes</u> is all it is.

My Grandma Nelle

Christine M. Kendall

My Grandma Nelle lived in Fishtown when fishermen lived there,
long before the hippies and artists moved in to make it their place.
My Grandma Nelle was a story teller, she made them up—
wrote poetry, played piano, lived simply, so she could clean her house
in an hour or less. She needed time for her writing,
including letters to friends; and in Fishtown on the Skagit,
long after Simon drowned, she lived with Clarence an Indian man,
but it was short-lived.

Clarence had a rocking chair which would creak, creak, creak,
when he was home rocking—not one to be still—
and the noise drove Nelle crazy, along with living out there
in the boonies where all the talk was about fish—catching them,
not catching them, almost catching them, and eating them
morning, noon, and night.

One day when Nelle's man was off fishing, in a fit of
had it *up to here* with a little vengeance thrown in,
she sawed off the rockers of his chair, walked out of Fishtown
and that was that.

Evening

Judith Azrael

The fishermen

folding their golden nets

and a faint breeze

carrying the scent of thyme

and oregano and roses

The hours have walked away

and the sea goes on singing

Checking the Boat at Night
In a Storm

Samuel Green

Because anchors let go their grip,
shackles wear, lines part, you rise when wind
becomes too loud to bear & slide out of bed
without waking your wife.

Because your wife still sleeps you dress
without light by the kitchen door, chore
boots & oilskins, watch cap & gloves,
& let yourself out into the dark.

Because it's dark, you carry
an old-fashioned lantern, the squeak
of its handle lost in gusts that sound
like runaway trucks, the harsh cracks
of limbs giving up, letting go.

Because limbs are tumbling
onto the roads & trails,
you should not take the shortcut
through the timber, but you do,
pushing the small pool of light
before you, eyes on the muddy duff,
crawling under one windfall fir
& the fresh wreck of an old madrone,
until rain becomes a sideways slash.

Because the rain hits your face
full on, you know you're out
of the woods beside Phil's hay
field, & you lean into the storm downhill
to find the old road that follows the bluff
above the dark bulk of the bay,

the pounding of breakers as loud
now as wind, metallic shriek of the ramp
pitching as the float bucks & slams into pilings
at the county dock, beside which you stop,
water breaking to the tops of your boots
before sucking the loose pebbles back.

Because everything is down to a few shades
of black, it does no good to look. A hundred yards
offshore your dory is riding the swells like a gull
as they roll beneath it, or it is already
kindling farther up the beach.

This is what you know: you filed the bow
thimble clean, made the eye splice tight.
In scuba gear you set the anchor yourself
in the muddy bottom, a Danforth, flukes
dug in, shaft facing the shore, tightened
the shackle pins, checked each link
of the chain to the nylon line, left plenty of scope
for tide or weather, kept it clean of mussels
& seaweed. The buoy was firm & floated high.
Your painter was new, strong, & tied with a bowline.

You knew all this before you left your bed—
that all that might be done you did. Yet here you are,
holding watch where you can't tell wind from surf,
salt spray from rain. Because. Because. Because again.

From A Journal

Denali National Park

John Morgan

Woke to heavy rain, low clouds,
the wet-rag sky wrung out
with little hope for change,

but since it's the park, we go.
And driving toward Wonder Lake,
the rain does change—to snow.

There on a hillside, a mother
grizzly playing with her cub—
delighted with each other

and by the frosty white,
they roll and wrestle in it.
At Eielson, a snowball fight

pits kids against the giddy bus
dispatcher. We take a hike.
And later hike again near

Stony Creek, noting a mound
of grizzly scat beside
a stretch of torn up ground

where the ravenous bear
rummaged turf for
ground squirrels—earth

gouged, mined, ripped, rocks
tossed aside like
ping-pong balls, a thorough

Morgan, con't.

thrashing of the region.
Wild nature on a tear
alters our perspective (after

the playful grappling of
mother and cub) on the crushing
strength and menace of a bear.

Quelcid, S'Klallam Elder, Teaches Us
Richard Lee Harris

Quelcid, S'Klallam elder, teaches us to make walking sticks. She beats her deerskin drum and sings: *Pick a devil's club, peeled and cured, that fits your stature. Bone it with a table knife, as my ancestors did with a deer's shoulder blade. Wrap the grip with rawhide. Hang on it amulets of rosehips and beads.*

To touch diabolical devil's clubs, *Oplopanax horridum*, causes me to shudder. With each stroke of the table knife I remember horse-logging with Dad and my brother Jim on the back of our place. I remember swamping out trails through devil's club and vine maple before each tree was felled and whacking out horse trails to drag the logs to the truck.

I remember Jim bending a green stem as I swung my ax. He let go. Up it sprang, slapping thorns into each of us, driving them through our worn-out gloves and into our hands. Always, when we'd stop to dig stingers out, dad and the team showed up, impatient and disgusted.

From Prince William Sound, to Vancouver Island, to Puget Sound, for centuries, indigenous people have burnt, carved, ground, painted, rubbed, steamed, tattooed, and infused roots, stems, inner bark, and berries of this ginseng, with thistles, black hawthorn, prince's pine, cascara, and bear grease for medicine, magic, and fishing lures.

And now to the beat of her drum, Quelcid sings: *Take*

your walking stick. Go quietly through shadowy thickets to the river's edge. Listen for its inner spirit speaking to a shaman, his face painted with bear grease and ash. Evil spirits know its magic, they will sneak away.

Olympic Peninsula, Washington, 1998

How The Motmot Got That Tail

Peggy Shumaker

When Sibo asked
every creature to help
make the world,

the motmot
hid
in a hole.

All the other animals,
all the other birds,
did their share.

A tattler saw
the motmot's tail,
plucked out one feather

then another. All the birds
chipped in, plucked.
Tired out just before they finished.

When the world was complete,
Sibo gave the birds a rest.
Motmot showed up, bragged

I did more than
all of you put together!
But his tail

testified.
He could not hide
his lazy behind.

And Still
Judith Azrael

This is a land of dust and tears and laughter

where all our lost dreams

are holding hands

this is a land of forgotten poems

all our words skipping away

like stones into the sea

I Don't Remember

Nancy Canyon

the smell of flakes falling from soggy clouds like wet towels pinned on a clothesline, nor the muffled squeals of children dancing through swirls and drifts at dusk. I don't remember the smell of fur-lined boots tossed inside a bootbox along with snow crusted mittens, wool scarves, and knit hats. I don't remember rosy cheeks burning in a steamy kitchen, nor miniature marshmallows melting in mugs of hot cocoa while sleds drip in the garage. I don't remember the sound of Daddy stumbling over a pile of boots that didn't make it into the bootbox, nor his words: *Leave that white crap outside where it belongs.*

Baja Healing

Rosalyn Ostler

In winter I come, hurting, to this place,
this sleepy summer village by the sea.
An illness, stress corroding inner space,
have overloaded, spent, and broken me
beyond ability to manage pace.
I hoped that coming here might set me free.
And then this sea of indigo and teal
astounds my eyes, and I begin to heal.

The sunlight glistens fronds of palm,
and bougainvillea overflows each lane.
I press my face into the fuchsia balm,
and flowers' touch relieves the buried pain.
A mourning dove above me chants a psalm;
its coo ca-roo coo-coo is dawn's refrain.
The flickers call from palo verde trees;
an unknown fragrance scents the sunny breeze.

The pelicans and frigate birds soon fly
the thermals, dive for fish, and rend
a clear expanse of morning-glory sky.
Wild horses running toward the beach descend
the sand, and cattle walking calmly by
on village streets in search of food, extend
the memory of freedom lost, restore
it while I stroll along this scalloped shore.

In shorts and barefoot, I touch golden sand
and, like Antaeus, feel revived again.
The rhythms of the rolling surf demand
no effort from me, simply ebb and then
take grief in cleansing flow. I understand
that I am well enough to take my pen
once more and free the feelings through the words
that swell and lift like songs of morning birds.

Ostler, con't.

A caucus—vultures perch *el cardons*,
their wings spread open wide as if to bless.
The air holds peace. I breathe it to my bones,
and sunlight warms my blood to wholesomeness.
Before the dawn, I walk to mounded stones
where I can wait for light to opalesce.
A skyline band of gold intensifies;
in awe, I watch the sun completely rise.

Aunt Mabel Talks About The Change

Sally Green

It was the hot flashes
bothered me most. It felt as though
a little of me shed
each time one struck, sudden-
like. Brought to mind summer cloud
bursts over the farm, the kind that left
a skim of moisture over everything.

Elmer moved into the extra bedroom
so I wouldn't worry over keeping him
awake nights what with throwing
the covers off one minute, pulling them on
the next. He minded my needs,
bless his big-hearted soul, the way
he babied those tea roses that lined the walk
to our front door.

Woman troubles weren't talked about
much when I was growing up. Now I think
of Mother and Mrs. Nelson and Mrs. Bertch
around our kitchen table and know
what was being chewed over. Youngsters
weren't allowed to listen to grown-up talk
so I curled myself up tight at the end
of the parlor sofa nearest the kitchen
door, my ear cupped for sounds
of leave-taking. I wanted a piece
of Mother's famous *kaffe kuchen*
she always had on hand when women
gathered. It was then I heard those phrases—
*nervous breakdown, the change, hot
flashes*—slither under the door.

Sally Green, con't.

On a prairie farm it was natural
to fatten up, take on a stoop. Skin
would get the wrinkles. Everyone
had some sort of ache
in the joints. But how all those women
managed a farm and family with reason
muddied-up like flooded grain
fields, spells of weariness bogging them down
like boots stuck in gumbo, and those bothersome
night sweats baffles me. Tougher stock
than I am! Those times I longed for nothing
more than a hole to crawl into, afraid
I was headed for the county asylum.

One thing those womenfolk had
was hand-me-down remedies. Herbs were plentiful
and filled many a jar shelved near
the stove. Mornings I watched Mother
make a tea she sipped throughout the day.
Whether they worked or not, those ladies
were what is now called a "support group."
They did what they could
with what they had. No such thing
as HRT and the doctors
weren't much help. How could a man understand
such symptoms? *All in the head*
was the popular notion.

It took my own change to teach me
why the preacher's wife hid when callers came,
why my best friend's mamma left for a "rest,"
but especially why Mother struck out
at her passel of kids for the tiniest things.
If it'd been talked about like matters get beat
into the ground nowadays, I'd have been less
shamed, more patient.

When Mother passed, one of the things that came
to me was the skin of a snake. I don't remember

seeing it, ever. She must have kept it
in the bedroom where we weren't allowed
to go. It's the color of washed-out milk,
a foot long, and thin as a pencil. Not like
any of the snakes on our farm. Through the toughest
times, that fragile sheath—its scales, beady eye
holes, unhinged jaws—got me through. I keep it
right over there, coiled around a rock atop a piece
of barn wood on Mother's desk. It looks a bit
like one of those Chinese souvenirs carved
from ivory. I keep it there to remind me
how sometimes we learn who we are
by what we leave behind, right up
to that last little wiggle. You know?

Wheatridge Care Center

Randy Phillis

Even though she's better than 80,
survived the Depression and did a man's work
during the big war, covered the Kansas oil fields
in a trailer caravan, was widowed young,
reared children and cats and dogs and turtles
and ended up alone to carry on all the business herself
after the hip replacements.
Even after the quadruple bypass she would still
drive 600 miles just to make a visit,
she feels herself blush a bit when Big James
at the nursing home picks her right up
like nothing out of the wheelchair and sits
her in the front seat of the van, saying
C'mon miss, you make me laugh so
I want you to ride shot-gun today
if you promise not to tell the boss,
and she's so flattered
she giggles and shakes a little, pretty sure
it's all a bit immodest, if not just plain indecent.

moving day

at the retirement home

my elderly friend

can't see

the red-winged blackbird

—*Andrew Shattuck McBride*

Dad, Belly Up

C.M. Clarke

She'd never seen her father shirtless before
rounded white belly up,
beached on the extra bed
unresponsive

Pin point eyes
slow breaths, floundering.
Medics hook him with IVs
pull him back from the icy blue water

Of Atlantic Ocean, hot sand of Jones Beach
and cotton candy Coney Island.
He lands in Harborview like a marlin braced
against all restraint.

He sobs apologies, tears spill down wrinkled waterways
and crease his gown
into the shady terrain of Doherty Creek
where father and daughter are first-time fishing.

She reels one in
and holds it in her hands,
too stunned by its shimmer
to decide its fate,

Until fate finally steps in,
looks at her with one milky blue eye
and he floats, belly up
hurtling downriver without her.

Driving Dad to The Dog Museum
Gailmarie Pahmeier

On cross country road trips, my father sang,
old songs he made us learn at least to hum,
my mother snapping along in the front seat,
their daughters untethered in the back.
He sang Oh, Susanna, he sang There's a Hole
In the Bucket, *dear Liza, dear Liza,*
he sang Maybellene *(why can't you be true?),*
songs with pet names for all of us.
Today I've sprung him from Assisted Living,
a picnic in the park, then the Dog Museum.
I'll pay to see the Huneck exhibit,
the wood cuts and chairs, admire
the exquisite porcelain Great Dane,
a harlequin. My father's done well
with his therapy dogs, their soft coats
bring back his days of raising hounds,
a young father, before the suits and ties,
before the suburbs. He loves best the room
which houses the war dogs exhibit,
old Rin Tin Tin and the Yorkie, Smoky.

As we enter the parking lot, circle
for a spot his chair can handle,
he starts to sing, he sings *Way Down Yonder
in the Land of Buttons*…he sings loudly,
his voice echoes across the lot, reaches
a woman walking her whippet, she's startled,
the dog turns toward us. My father
ignores the woman, says i*sn't that the same dog
your friend had in high school? Wasn't she the one
who died of a self-inflicted woe?
What happened to her dog? Was he sad, too?*
Before I can begin to answer,
my father starts to sing, he sings This Old Man—

Pahmeier, con't.

knick knack paddywack, give the dog a bone!
This old man came rolling home. By the time
we travel the museum's ramp, he has sung
all ten verses, twice, and I'm Liza again, mending.

Spring Burial in the Sandhills
Neil Harrison

After the service and the slow procession,
a multi-hued line of pickups and cars,
mini-vans and SUVs, all moving west
from the church and south into the hills,

the pastor's voice at the gravesite
sweeps east on the April wind,
as the far trilling of cranes drifts down,

a carnival helix of the great wild birds
spiraling upward far to the west,
winged escort singing you
up from the season of planting and birth,

out of the skein of time,
where what is here consigned to the earth
has already flowered.

Ghosts

Bruce Douglas Reeves

"**G**oddam it! You're trying to kill me!"

I can't be sure, any more, if I shouted that before or after I crawled under the coffee table, but I know it was pretty far along into the twenty-four encounter group. Eight of us, four couples, had actually paid someone to facilitate this ordeal. Back then, encounter groups were considered a certain way to discover the weaknesses and strengths of any relationship. Here, we had multiple relationships, a three-dimensional chess game of relationships, to sort out. The eight of us had been babbling for two years about forming a commune, another surefire path to peace and contentment, but hadn't got very far, so we'd decided that we needed to break the log jam. It broke it, all right. After this, we went our separate ways.

I know that I crept under the coffee table at about this point in the fun and games, and slid into my own twilight zone, where pondered without interference the personal relationships about which the facilitator and several of the others had become obsessed. They didn't understand, they had no clue....

***

"No, goddam it! You're trying to kill me!"

When my Aunt Libby's great heart wore out, my father turned his bony back on the idea of returning to the city of his birth for her funeral. Although he'd loved Libby for three-quarters of a century with the awe and tenderness of a younger brother, his excuses piled up until they became a fortress behind which he crouched like the urchin in short pants he'd once been.

"I can't leave Louise," he protested. "And god knows she can't go."

Of course, he didn't ask my mother if she felt well enough to go with him, or even if she wanted to escape her airless nest for a few hilarious days of mourning and reminiscence. Parents. Family. Two of the more lethal words in the English language.

Also, he admitted, after so many years at sea level he didn't trust his old organs to Utah's unforgiving altitude. "I'd make it a double funeral," he predicted, but with the merciless presumption of the young I assured him that Lourdes and I would watch out for Mom, that he was tough as a Clydesdale, and for that matter wasn't old.

Lifting his bushy white eyebrows, he barked back, "Wait 'til you're seventy-five, my boy, and see if you think it's old, or not."

Finally, he admitted with a dip of his knobby, almost hairless head that he was terrified of trading the security of Mother Earth for the unpredictability of a flying tin can. Sylvester belonged to one of the first generations to grow up worshiping the motor car. He dated events in his life with the auto he or his family owned at the time: "That was when we had the Graham-Paige touring car," or, "You remember, it was just after I bought the Plymouth coupe...."

Automobiles he knew and understood, but he had never inserted his body into any machine that left the ground and didn't intend to, now.

"There's nobody in Utah I want to see, anyway. Or who wants to look at this ugly face."

The hollows and crevices that framed his features froze in boyish defiance.

Our clan was large and my father still resented many, perhaps most, of those stepbrothers and stepsisters, nieces and nephews, cousins, and other relations who still cluttered the western United States. He still believed that each of them had played a part in propelling him into what he called the smash up of his life. This was a man who held grudges like slivers of ice in his lard-encased heart and intended to haul them to his grave, where perhaps they'd finally thaw. The poison from those shards of frozen pain had bled through his system all those years, souring his life and tainting the lives of us who loved him.

"If I leave here," he croaked, "I'll never get back alive."

"But what about Aunt Libby and Uncle Frank? They weren't scared."

I was cheating, now, and we both knew it. The fact was that his older sister and her husband hadn't been afraid to fly. Just two years before, both of them leaning toward eighty, they'd allowed a cut rate regional airline to transport them from Salt Lake City over the Sierras to Oakland. My parents didn't have space for my aunt and uncle in their one-bedroom bat cave of an apartment and my mother would've slept in a dumpster rather than in the same building with Libby, so they ended up with Lourdes and me in Berkeley. However, mentioning Libby and Frank's visit turned out to be a tactical error.

Ruddy-faced, white-haired Frank had seemed as handsome and virile as ever—as long as he sat silently on his cushioned throne—but whenever he tried to walk or to push a few words past his lips he was exposed as a shuffling, slurring semi-invalid, the legacy of a recent stroke. Nevertheless, Libby, after nearly sixty years of marriage, continued as always to treat him as if he were the Sun King. A short, dumpy figure of affectionate concern, she was two-thirds deaf by then, but she smiled at what she couldn't hear, shouted back at anybody who tried to communicate with her, and went about her business—which, in her mind, primarily was to serve her man's needs. My father had been devastated by Frank's abrupt decline not only because he remembered Frank as a powerful young athlete, but also because he had no doubt that his brother-in-law's deterioration foreshadowed his own.

"I was twelve when Libby and Frank were married," he told me, one night after they slowly dragged their bulky bodies to my guest room. "He taught me everything I know about fishing and hunting. He had a motorcycle then—nineteen-twenty-two, that'd be—and he took me all over hell on it. During the Depression, I bunked for a while with Libby and Frank. They kept me alive when I thought I might as well be dead. I couldn't love Frank more if he was my own flesh and blood."

However, it was bustling, tireless Libby whose heart gave out first. It was her funeral my father was scared to face. He knew how he'd find Frank and saw no need to endure it, any more than he wanted to confront his other relatives after years of recriminations and blame.

"I know it's my last chance to see 'em," he said, staring into the sudsy dregs of his evening beer. "My own kin. The last chance I'll have." He took a gulp, leaving foam on his lips. "But who says I wanna see 'em, anyway?"

At last, I offered to go with him: a simple gesture, but as safe as it was facile. I'd grown up, after all, with this man and his titanic stubbornness. I knew he'd never change his mind. My mother would give up her tranquilizers and pain killers before he'd agree to go back to the mountainous, holier-than-thou land where he was born and raised. But he brought his leathery face close to mine, and, as if he'd been waiting for my offer, agreed.

"I'll go, but I'll die. You'll see. You'll be stuck with a corpse, but I'll go."

For the next thirty-six hours, he complained about the aggravation of traveling and the effort of getting ready, bemoaned the strain of preparing my mother to cope without him, and repeatedly let me know that he felt bullied and manipulated.

I dreaded the coming days of enforced company with my father, days that would be filled with old landmarks, fragments of his and therefore my history, and rehashing of familiar tales. We'd share tears along the way: tears of anger, regret, and pain. In our family, we don't suffer silently; we shout and weep and complain, often blurting accusations too hurtful to be forgiven. Still, I charged the tickets, helped him pack, reassured him and consoled my mother, and finally escorted him onto the plane, while our wives stayed behind to comfort and be comforted.

To Dad, the multi-hued plastic decor and semi-reclining chairs of economy class spelled luxury, intimidating him as much as the prospect of flying had scared him. Struggling to be a good sport, he rolled his eyes at a frazzled flight attendant and whispered to me that if he'd known the stewardesses were so cute he'd have flown before, but his usually pink face faded to gray as the plane taxied down the runway and when it tilted and began straining upward, his skull pressed rigidly against the seat back and his eyes focused their full, fierce attention on the geometric shapes woven into the fabric in front of them.

We stayed with my uncle in the yellow frame house he shared with Libby for so many years. I remembered that bungalow and the country lane in front of it. The summer of 1952, during my often unsettled childhood, my parents and I camped there while my father tried to decide where he wanted to cart his family next. I slept on the living room sofa that August, so I ended up watching large hunks of the Democratic National Convention on the squat television set in the corner. Half-dozing, as I waited for the grownups to clear out of my makeshift bedroom, I absorbed the sweaty gray and white carnival atmosphere of the old fashioned political powwow. Those politicians behaved almost as erratically and noisily as my relations.

Although as a kid I had little basis for comparison (we always rented when I was growing up—duplexes, apartments, semi-detached houses), now I saw how small Frank and Libby's two-bedroom place actually was. It didn't even have a dining room; my aunt and uncle ate in the kitchen or on TV trays in the living room. This wasn't the house where they'd raised their two kids, but—bought for two thousand bucks from Frank's brother, Sam, after World War Two—it was the only home they ever owned.

My father and I maneuvered among the bulky shapes of half-recognized relatives and lemon-waxed mismatched furniture, whispering out of respect for (or fear of) the memories that clung like dust to each table, chair, and curtain. A color television loomed on a spindly-legged stand in the corner where the 1952 black and white model had stood. Crumbling, silver-maned Frank sprawled like a felled Titan on a lumpy overstuffed chair, tears pooled in the craters of his red face. Seeing him there was like gazing on Mt. Rushmore after it had been devastated by lightning.

Sylvester muttered half-swallowed greetings at his relatives, but they refused to look at him eye-to-eye, peering sideways, as if he were a rattler coiled to strike. Grabbing me by the arm, he dragged me out the back door. The instant we stumbled onto the little back porch and confronted the wading pool-sized lawn and overgrown flower beds, a wave of memories slapped me in the face. I remembered that little yard and the peeling patio furniture better than I did the house.

Whenever we visited my aunt and uncle during my childhood, I hung out alone back there among the haphazard greenery and shimmering fireflies while the adults tossed back beers or highballs inside and complained about the arrogant way the Mormon elders ran the state. Squinting, I could imagine the glimmer of fireflies above spindly rose bushes and randomly pruned hedges on a summer evening, recall the thrill of handling the variegated stones and broken geodes collected by Libby and Frank on their rock hunting expeditions into the Utah desert, and feel my excitement when Libby demonstrated how she used the foot treadle-operated rock polisher she kept in the shed behind the garage.

But Dad refused to linger in the yellow cottage and miniature garden. He needed to escape this pious crowd and follow other trails from the past, listen to other, perhaps more congenial, voices whispering from the dark canyons of memory. He wasn't a sophisticated man, but he knew that these people so busy saying all the right words that expressed all the proper sentiments, didn't feel a goddam thing about the loss of Libby, his sister, damn it, and one of the best women who ever walked this miserable piece of real estate.

"There're too damn many people in that house," he told me, his false teeth clicking in that way he had when he'd tolerate no argument. "I can't breathe."

Who could blame him? Looking back, I see that our family was an encounter group, an encounter group through time and space, complaining, quarreling, challenging, demanding, insisting, and even, sometimes, loving. It was enough to wear out anybody.

While our shuffling, noisy relatives made appropriate mournful noises at each other within the cramped rooms, we drove our rented Ford into the city to let my father pursue the shadows, if not the substance, of his youth. Ghosts chased our shiny sedan, but other ghosts were waiting, as well. First, we headed out South Main, although he knew his grandmother's high-hipped red brick house—the home he was raised in—hadn't stood there for decades. Progress had destroyed much of this part of Salt Lake City. In certain strategic ways, the Mormon fathers clung to the past, but when it was profitable, my father always said, they embraced modern times, all right. Nostalgia did damn little for the bottom line.

"*This* was a dirt road," he told me, as we navigated the relentless currents of Salt Lake City traffic. His skimpy still-black hair was smeared across his damp scalp like so many India ink scrawls and his old eyes strained, almost trying to escape the pockets of loose skin that held them as they gazed at the changed city. "Mud when it rained, dust and dirt the rest of the time. In the fall, we built bonfires in the street—piles, mountains, of leaves flamin' and smokin' into the night."

Shiny glass and steel cliffs had long ago crowded into the old neighborhood, reflecting the traffic that rushed where Sylvester and his siblings and cousins once played. Yet even I remembered the old house, with its pair of linden trees and wide front lawn spilling down to the sidewalk. Although I came along much too late to race or play ball in the unpaved street of his youth, I'd rolled on the sloping grass here, explored the sheltered porch that stretched the width of the house, and been frightened by the dark cellar windows blinking below, the sightless eyes of a blinded giant. I was just a little grub, then, but I remembered the place better than the people, or felt that I did.

I was a little scared sometimes when we went there, scared of the wide sheltered porch and its dark shadows and the black cellar windows blinking at me, the sightless eyes of a blinded giant. A hungry giant. He could crawl out from under the house and eat me. Daddy told me that the people who lived in that big house were family.

Now, scratching at the debris of memory, I recalled dimly lit rooms and dark-grained furniture that towered and swayed above me. Pictures formed in my head, illustrating stories that I didn't know existed there. I remembered a young woman—my father's half-sister, Iris, a near-sighted teenager at the time, wide-hipped already, but not the stout pillar of the Mormon Church she later became. She babysat me sometimes. She wasn't scared of that house. Or of the shadows. Not even the giant in the basement. And I wasn't scared of her.

I liked it when my aunt Iris sat with me at the piano, her protective arm holding me on the long bench as we plonked out patchwork tunes. It was a big old upright made of dark wood and boasted a polished brass candle sconce on each side. Other times, she played tunes just for me. She lifted up the top of the piano bench and took out sheets of paper with squiggles over them that told her how to play the tunes. Some squiggles were for white keys and some squiggles were for black keys. Sometimes, she held my hand so I could plunk out music, too. We called the song "Chopsticks." I didn't know what that meant. It sounded silly, a made up word, but it was fun. Not scary.

She taught me the ABCs. Letters. They were on my wood blocks, letters that stuck out so my fingers could trace their shapes. The red "A" block had an apple on the other side. The blue "H" block had a horse. The yellow "C" block had a clown—the clown had a scary smile. I didn't like it. The clown looked mean. He lived in the shadows.

"Don't be silly! It's only a picture on a block, a piece of wood." That was my Dad. He scared me, too, sometimes.

"Letters," Aunt Iris said, "make words."

Maybe, but I didn't know how to do that. I imagined letters tossed into the air and falling around me, falling onto the floor and making a picture, like the pieces of my jigsaw puzzle. Mom and Dad and other grownups sent words flying over my head and around me and through me. I talked sometimes, when I didn't feel shy, but most of the time the grownups didn't hear my words. When you're big enough, words are like magic: nothing stops them. I imagined that the bugs at night were words, buzzing words, darting and flying. Could words sting?

"Too damn much imagination," my daddy said. "That kid has too much imagination."

And wasn't that *me* in a slate-floored kitchen with a skinny old lady—undoubtedly my father's stepmother—munching fingers of toast she cooked on a huge black stove? I didn't know who she was, then, but she was in that house when Daddy took me there. He didn't seem to like her very much. When we went there and saw the old lady, he made faces at my mom and she whispered back at him. The old lady didn't see, but I did. Other figures drifted through that old house, too, ghosts all, specters from another age and time. They still haunted my father then and haunt me, now. A man lived in that house, but I hardly ever saw him. He was my father's Daddy. I didn't know why I didn't see him more. Maybe he was hiding. Shadows were black spots that hid things...and people, sometimes. That house was full of black spots. Shadows.

My visits to that old-fashioned house standing like a dowager on its ample lot ended suddenly when my father quarreled with his stepmother. By the time I was old enough to collect conscious memories, my grandfather was dead, leaving behind two sets of children and a sickly second wife.

I have a photograph of my grandfather, father, and me looking like the stoical carvings on a totem pole planted in the sloping front lawn, but the sepia image is of three strangers: a plump toddler at the bottom, two grinning men stacked above his chipmunk face. Holding the photo up to the light, today, I feel regret, but little else. I don't remember my grandpa and that muscular young fellow in the snapshot scarcely suggests the man I've known as my Dad, but the faded fragment of brick wall and patch of grass behind them produce a twinge of nostalgia. I remember those bricks, that lawn—or think I do. A tattered remnant of my own past hangs on that setting, even if the human shadows in front evade meaning.

"My grandmother built the house with money she brought from England," Sylvester announced as we drove to the spot where it once stood. "Her brothers gave it to her. Those Wilcox boys did okay for themselves, but they never forgot their sister—even after she was in America." He grimaced: "It was always her house, never Grandpa's, never the family's. Hers."

"That old gal was tough," he said, with an undertone, even after so many years, of both awe and fear.

Isobel Wilcox dominated her husband, her son, even her grandchildren, for as long as she lived. She drove away her son's first wife—my beautiful, ambitious grandmother —and terrorized his second wife. Although a fervent Latter Day Saint, as only a convert can be, she stubbornly consumed her endless cups of strong English tea. Even the Mormon church had to compromise with Isobel Wilcox.

"The old witch controlled the family purse strings 'til she croaked. When my father tried to move his family to

California, she made such a stink he gave up. That's why my mother left him."

"Taking you with her."

"Yeah. Taking me with her."

The ghosts of those two women facing off in that red brick house haunted us still: old Isobel and her daughter-in-law, Adelaide. Wilful and impetuous, dark-haired Adelaide was no match for her husband's mother. How much of my father's personality was formed by that old woman from Leeds, and by extension how much of my own?

Nudging our rental sedan against the high granite curb in front of a hardware store's glass and tile facade, we gazed past the cars and buses to the other side where once stood the red brick home of a young married couple from England's Midlands. It was difficult to imagine the lawns or solid houses that lined this wide boulevard then. A common wisecrack was that you could get sunstroke crossing a Salt Lake City street on a summer day, and it must've seemed so even more when Sylvester was a boy and the unpaved street wasn't confined by either sidewalks or curbs.

"Grandpa ended up a letter carrier," Dad murmured, staring with folded arms into the magic box of memory. "He wanted to be an artist, but when I knew him he drove a horse-drawn mail wagon. I loved his brown mare. When Grandpa stopped for lunch, he put the feed bag around her neck and took out his sandwich and they ate together, wherever they happened to be. I went with him, sometimes. If I close my eyes, I can still smell the oats in the feed bag."

Standing at that intersection, held back by speeding cars and aggressive buses and delivery trucks, we pictured the bony, wide-rumped mare munching her oats while my spectacled great grandpa, a slim, dapper man with a carefully trimmed, pointed beard, sat in the wagon eating a bacon sandwich wrapped in oiled paper.

"Damn!"

Blinking furiously, my father slapped his leg with his open palm and turned his back on both the street and the memories and ghosts he found there. "Better Than Paint!" declared a six-foot banner splashed behind a plate glass window in the store next to us.

"The Greens lived on this side," he said, his voice so hoarse that I had to lean forward to catch the words as they fell from his damp lips. "Aunt Priscilla and my cousin Wilfred were there." He pointed to a tall brick house that now existed only in memory and in a few antique photographs: "Across the street from my grandmother's place. The two spinsters, Clara and Grace, lived next door, with their brother, Tod. None of 'em ever married."

Judge and jury of both the past and the shadows who lived there, he confronted the ghostly defendants who swarmed around him.

"When Uncle Tod died, everything he had went to his sisters. And he had plenty to leave, 'cause as a young man he'd been to the gold fields in California. That was what everybody said."

My father stood next to me on that sidewalk, but he

wasn't there. He was watching two small, plainly dressed middle-aged spinsters go about their daily business. One was taller, one was stouter, one had graying hair before the other, both of them wore that hair coiled into a bun at the back of the head. One took the streetcar to the school where she taught, returning in the afternoon, carrying papers to correct. The other stayed home. Whatever went on in their heads, they revealed none of it, not so their nephew could ever see it.

My father paced the wide sidewalk, staring into store windows crowded with holiday decorations, although it was only early November, but he was looking beyond those paper bells and plastic garlands, into the insubstantial world of the past.

"Clara was the quiet one. Never did anything on her own—just kept house for her sister. Grace was a school teacher. In those days, women teachers couldn't marry and keep their jobs. They had another brother, too. My uncle Walter. Another bachelor. He shot himself with a pearl-handled revolver he kept at home. Nobody knew why, as far as I ever heard. But, hell, I was only a kid at the time."

Was Dad talking to himself or to me? How could either of us know? Maybe I hadn't been as considerate as I'd thought I was, pushing him to come back here after all this time. Maybe it was harder for him than I'd imagined it could be.

The youngster I'd seen in photos, costumed in miniature World War One dough boy garb, complete with putties: was that the kid who wondered about Walter Green's suicide? Or was it the youth in knee britches and soft cap, standing cockily, one hip out and a smart ass expression on his round face? And what do either of those boys have to do with this angry, anguished, deeply creased face next to me on this Salt Lake City curb?

"All of Walter and Tod's money funneled down to those two spinsters. When Clara died, she left everything to Grace. That one must've ended up a millionaire, but she kept teaching 'til the school board made her retire. I don't think that old female miser liked anybody—besides her damn cats, I mean."

My father glared at the pavement, his face a relief map of frustration and disappointment. His old black shoes, polished for the trip, shuffled on the curb, as he took several panting breaths. Was he waiting for my reaction? No, maybe I was an audience, but one from whom nothing but silence was expected or wanted.

"Everybody in the family thought they'd get some of Grace's dough, but she surprised 'em all. Not that I expected a goddam penny. I knew better'n that."

He saw me looking at him and frowned, a crease between his eyes deepening the canyons of loose flesh around them, and giving him a sleepy look, as if the altitude and excitement and emotional stress were going to send him to bed. Maybe that would've been a good idea, but the memories wouldn't stop.

"I'll tell you why, I knew. Goddam it, I'll tell you."

I started to say that it wasn't necessary, that maybe we should go someplace where he could rest, but another look from those eyes shut me up quick.

"It was a Saturday during the Depression, when I was out of work. Hell, almost everybody was out of work. Grace asked me to drive her 'round town, shopping, paying bills, that kind of thing. She had a little black coupe—looked like an old-fashioned top hat, and not much bigger. I was glad to do it—didn't get to do much driving then. So I chauffeured Aunt Grace around Salt Lake all afternoon, waited for her to do her errands, then took her home. When I gave the car keys back to her, she reached into a little jet-covered purse and pulled out a dollar bill. 'Here, Sylvester,' she said. But I shook my head. 'I don't want any money, Aunt Grace,' I said. 'I enjoyed driving you 'round.' A buck was a lot of money, then, too. A man would work all day for a dollar. Then she pursed her lips together and shoved the bill back at me, ordering me to take it—but, damn it, I wouldn't. I could be stubborn, too. Grace never spoke to me again. She couldn't forgive me for not taking her stinkin' dollar. And what did she do but leave all her money to the goddam animal shelter. Nobody in the family got a dime. That was during the Depression and a little money could've changed my life, but not a cent."

His yellowish features trembled—with rage, regret, weariness—until they looked as if they were starting to melt. An image flashed into my brain from a long-ago movie in which the flesh fell from a man's face, leaving only a pale skull. Usually, when Dad talked about his family, he shouted and condemned, as if shoving his fury at me could make a difference, but now grief and pain slid like silent shadows over his face, leaving their residue among the furrows I knew so well. Sometimes, it seemed that life was just too hard—why should it be so damn hard?

A breeze pushing up South Main chilled us as my father glared across the street at the piece of real estate where his English-born grandmother had ruled like the Red

Queen, never stopping to look either inward at her own motivation or outward at the effect her tyranny had on the lives of those around her. Then he farted, a loud, unexpected, raucous noise that startled both of us. His eyes opened wide and he laughed—a short, bray of a laugh.

"That's what the past is worth, son," he growled. "One stinky fart!"

In the days before pop-psychology, before whole forests fell to produce books and magazines that explained us to ourselves and before television became crowded with gurus and "personality" experts who dragged miserable slobs before our eyes and explained to them and to us why they were so messed up, before all that nonsense, people just plunged ahead with their lives, not doubting or questioning themselves, but believing that, for the most part, their existence was ruled by external forces Sylvester still operated this way, unable to look without prejudice into the convolutions of either past or present. He allowed himself no awareness of inner terrors, risked no analysis of behavior. He, like old Isobel Wilcox and the rest of her dead kin, believed in nothing that couldn't be explained by simple phrases, homilies, and "root-stock" values. Most of all, he believed in blame.

"I didn't get a goddam thing out of that house. Nothing from the sale and not much from inside it, either." He glared at the building that had replaced his grandmother's brick home. "Hester and her kids cheated me. Kept it all for themselves. My father would've wanted me to have his books, at least. But I only got one lousy little box."

For more than forty years, Dad resented his father's lost library. In his mind, he was cheated out of it, as he was cheated of so much, and anger was his only revenge. His false teeth, ill-fitting even on the best days, clacked and slid, garbling his words, but I knew the meaning of his oration, even if the particulars were lost in the battle between tongue and dentures. Exhausted, stunned with grief, he complained of hurts suffered decades ago. Was it too much to expect him to thrust the dead part of his life behind him and to live for this moment, while he could? Perhaps it was, and I'm not sure that I do it any better.

I've seen him hurl a whole cherry pie at the wall, seen him terrorize my mother with his rage (not at her but at the past) until she locked herself in the bathroom. I worried that he'd lurch into a furious jig on that street corner, his overweight body already strained by the unaccustomed altitude, but his spotted hand plucked a fistful of snapshots from his jacket pocket. He had snitched these small, yellowed photos from my aunt's albums.

"Nobody'll miss 'em," he said, with a satisfied smirk. The gray faces on those ancient snaps were eerily familiar to me, yet I couldn't name more than two or three of them.

Snapshots were important in our family. The great dynasties of Europe had their court painters, their walls and staircases of elegantly preserved, often flattered, faces. We had our albums and shoeboxes of snapshots and occasional studio portraits, black and white, sepia-hued, sometimes hand-tinted. The urge to preserve our likenesses for posterity continued. My mother was crazy for taking photographs and pasting the hideous results in albums, annoying and frequently infuriating her victims, but now we have those snapshots and can study them, not just to see the arrangement of features on each face, but to try to see beyond them, into the expression on the mouth, the light lurking in the eyes, the hope or fear or complacency that was part of each individual in our clan.

Standing beside my dad, I peered at the passersby who stared at him, at me, at both of us, as they walked, drove, cycled past, but Salt Lake City wasn't steel-hearted L.A. or self-centered San Francisco and I saw sympathy on their faces, even concern, although they could've had no notion of why this bald man with the weathered face was shaking and stamping on their immaculate sidewalk. Maneuvering my father into the rental car, I ferried him away from that corner, even if we couldn't escape the ghosts who lingered there.

We drove along the wide, tree-sheltered streets he knew long ago. The erratic spirals of his life had brought him back to where he started more than seven decades ago. And for what? Can any of us understand why we suffer? Yet, like a child who has pinched his finger in a door, we look around, holding the place that hurts, the question in our eyes: why? I saw it in my father's bruised, corrugated face that day. We were attacked by ghosts in Salt Lake City, but that was no surprise. The surprise was when I realized that we couldn't escape those specters from the past, and maybe we weren't supposed to escape them.

Seeking refuge at a café, we ordered wedges of pie to sooth our distress. Sylvester had always found comfort in food, especially in desserts.

"After Libby got out of high school," he told me, between bites of blueberry pie with chocolate ice cream (his favorite combination since childhood), "she went to work for the phone company. When she got her first pay check, she bought herself a fancy walking stick with a handle like a grinning fox. Walking sticks were the rage, then tall ones, with fancy carved wood or silver handles, if you could afford 'em. All the girls wanted to be elegant like Gloria Swanson and Bebe Daniels in the movies, with their goddam walking sticks. I needed money for books and tuition to stay in high school, but Libby had to buy her hand-carved walking stick."

At a table by the window, a young woman in a red dress and black sweater sipped from a steaming coffee mug. She puckered her lips and blew, then cradled the white mug in her hands, letting the steam rise against her pale skin. Sylvester seemed quite taken with this petit young female. Did she remind him of another delicate brunette beauty, the ever-popular Bebe Daniels? What, I wondered, would happen if I walked across that checkered floor and lifted her chin, so we both could peer beneath the damp veil of her lashes? But I only watched my father gaze at her, then adjust his teeth and finish his pie.

I wasn't here from duty, I reminded myself. I was here because I wanted to be—for love. And in my family, we all love each other. We proclaim our love frequently. No letter, no greeting, no farewell, can pass without a declaration of love. We consider this love both a necessity and a fact.

Dad looked up from his blueberry-smeared plate, focusing his devastated eyes on me. Then, carefully, as if this were a task he needed do just so, he rubbed first his right eye and then his left with the knuckle of his right forefinger. I didn't think he was smearing away tears, but I quickly paid the bill and dropped some quarters beside our coffee cups and plates. When I glanced again at the table by the window, only the young woman's mug and a crumpled paper napkin remained.

"I appreciate you bringing me back here," Dad mumbled, as he stood, brushing crumbs from his shirt front. "I don't want you to think I don't appreciate it." I nodded and we left the café. "And I ain't dead, yet," he added.

Aunt Libby's funeral, when we gathered for it, comforted no one. Like sleepwalkers, the aged and aging survivors of various branches of our far-flung clan shuffled in and out, surrounded by the guerilla forces of youth. The Church Bishop, a fleshy middle-aged man with a blunt nose and thick brows, assured Frank that he and Libby would be reunited for eternity, but my uncle's handsome head jerked sideways in an expression of disbelief. His old eyes, bright with tears, said eloquently that he didn't need or want fairytales, but looked forward to the nothingness that would end his pain.

Irritated by the droning banalities, I let my eyes wander around the big, high-ceilinged room. Passing clouds sent shadows through the tall, narrow windows, their blobby shapes drifting across the serious, bored, impatient faces. My thoughts during my aunt's funeral weren't of her or of my scattered encounters with her over the decades as much as they were of my father. Fragments of our lives collided in my head, exploding into surreal landscapes.

I saw myself not much higher than the tabletop, watching him sketch a pencil portrait of my mother, the quick careful lines astonishingly capturing her round girlish face, her petulant lips, her wide surprised eyes. Even then, I could see that his rendering showed her as a pretty but not particularly happy young woman. Like his grandfather, once he wanted to be an artist. Like his grandfather, he settled for another life.

I saw him later, staggering home half-drunk after work, shouting at my mother that if it weren't for her and his kids he'd put himself out of his misery, once and for all. "Remember that when you jump on me." A perplexed expression hovered on his scarred face, as if he had no idea how he'd ended up in that crowded duplex living room, tugging off those heavy, battered work shoes. "I'm sick of it," he muttered, "sick of it." And he passed out across the worn sofa, his tired body sprawled like that of a fallen warrior.

And I watched myself much later lifting him from a hospital bed, his body frail and his spirit mean as he cursed the injustice of old age. "Damn it, take your hands off me! Let the nurses do it. That's what they're paid for." And he punctuated his exclamations with obscene bodily noises, maybe deliberate, maybe not. Then, inexplicably, he winked, as if to say that this performance—and perhaps all his performances—was a joke, his own goofy acknowledgment of the screwball comedy of his life.

After Libby's funeral, we fled the massive wreck that was Uncle Frank and I took Dad back to California, to the woman who waited in two airless rooms. But, at least, they were together, as they had been for forty and more years, grumbling and weeping and proclaiming love for each other.

"Poor old Frank," my father kept saying. "Poor old Frank."

Where did that leave me? Facing my own terrors, just as my father finally confronted his terror of flying, his fear of the past, and his certainty that death waited in the land of his birth. At least, I had his example before me, as what? A warning? If only I could've turned off the memories as easily as Aunt Libby used to flick off her hearing aid.

* * *

Eventually, I crawled out from underneath the coffee table. I don't think I'd passed out or slept while I was there. I remember voices crossing over me, colliding above the glass and mahogany table, and feet shuffling on the carpet around me. Mostly, I was thinking about my father and my family and their—my—history. I'd tried to explain to these people, my friends, about who I was, how I got this way, and my family. I guess that was what each of us did during those sleepless twenty-four hours, but it was hopeless. We could vent, yell and scream, cry and wail, or wish we could, but none of it mattered. No wonder I crawled under the table.

Those feet, as I crept out from under the coffee table like a snail wiggling across the carpet, were blurry. In the dim morning light, through whatever liquid had collected in my eyes, shoes, naked toes, socks, sofa and chair legs, scattered fragments of bodies, all of them, were blurry. I wasn't just me, any more, I was part of something bigger, something that didn't need to constantly proclaim its love. Maybe I'd had my own private encounter group under that table, without even knowing it. Now, I rubbed a sleeve across my face and smiled, pretending that nothing had happened. It was a harmless lie, after all.

Santa Cruz Boardwalk

Stephanie Cosky Hopkinson

You wore your Yogi Bear t-shirt,
light blue and washed so thin
it would ruffle in the wind of a heavy sigh

'Better clench your toes,' you said, nodding at my flip flops
I clenched and my right flip flopped off
'Great. I'll get it right in the face.'

Our friends, already paired off
and screaming down the rail,
left the last little roller coaster car for us

We stepped into the metal car and sat
you in the back, resting your arms on the sides
me in the front, knees bent and toes clenched

The car jerked as it ratcheted up the first hill
I hung on to the sissy bars so I wouldn't slip back into your lap
'Sorry,' you said shifting your legs to give me more room

The car stopped at the top of the hill
and it seemed like we hung there forever
floating on the smell of oiled wood and popcorn

The beach slid from under the boardwalk into the soft surf
and the warm breeze blew sheets of grey across the sea
'Shark attack last year,' I said.

You tapped out a rhythm on the painted metal. 'Can't get us here.'
'Look! You can see our dorm!' I said.
'They can't get us there, either.'

Then we sat in silence and waited
I stared at the sea, you stared at the redwoods
You said, 'I think it's brok…'

Cosky Hopkinson, con't.

and with a metal squeal our car dropped,
we both grabbed for the sissy bars
and hung on in stoic silence

until momentum shoved us against the side of the car
and we shrieked in surprise
so then there was nothing to do but go for it

We screamed down each hill, howled at oncoming turns
and shouted out nonsense words on the straightaway.
'Your hair tastes like soap,' you yelled.

Then the end. The car slid to a gentle stop,
you hopped out to offer me a hand
and held it just a moment longer than necessary

You reached out and gave my shoulder a soft quick pat.
"That was fun," you said.
I tapped Yogi Bear with one finger. 'Yeah,' I said.

All I know about your life after that
comes from a terse notice in the paper—
name, job title and that final date

So I don't know what kind of man you became
or what kind of life you lived
But I hope you remembered that day

When we were young
Poised between sky and sand
Not quite touching,
not quite ready for the ride

—for Chuck, 1965 - 2012

Daffodils This Time, McLean Road Again

Samuel Green

All week children in the schools I visit
try to help me with *yellow*. How do I tell
my wife, back home on our island,
what it's like? *Take a picture* says one. No,
I say, what *I* see, not what the camera sees.

Es un amarillo tan brillante, says a girl, like butter
mi abuela melts on my toast. No,
says another, like the raincoat my father wears
in the fields. Maybe the lemon my mother slices
for shrimp soup. *Los ojos de nuestro perro,* those old
doggy eyes in the porchlight. Ripe corn just shucked.
La camisa de Mr. Shapiro, or Ms. Romero's pencil.
The way my mother laughs. The stripes
on a wasp, the one that stung me. A banana,
says another, because I'm hungry.

But I am thinking of the yellow lunchbox
I lost when I was nine working in the berry fields. Inside,
on sheets of paper, was the name of a girl written
two hundred precise times, a charm to make her love me
back. I never spoke to her again, afraid someone
found it & told. Ten times ten
thousand flowers, the color of absence,
silent, forthright, cold.

On the Loss of a Friend

Jon D. Lee

Such a silly worry:
the absence of a scant few trillion cells,
several pounds of carbon,
an ounce of magnesium,
a few feet of intestine.
Who would notice a missing leg,
an absent hand,
an empty stomach,
a misplaced heart?
Certainly not these people who surround me,
these ideations who move from sterile pocket to sterile pocket,
tripping over sidewalk cracks as they talk to their phones.
"Fuck," they say,
"It's only fucking Monday afternoon?"
As if the world owes them respite,
still holds the change from their purchase,
has somehow miscalculated the balance
between what has been given
and what has been taken away.

When Light is Narrowing

Rosalyn Ostler

When I am dying, cell by cell,
and barely see the narrowed light,
I'll still recall you kissed me well.

If there is little more to tell
of life, and even less of sight,
when I am dying, cell by cell,

I'll still remember how we fell
to love; and, with delight,
I'll still recall you kissed me well.

Though other memories can't compel
my thought or muster strength to fight,
when I am dying cell by cell,

this kiss will lift my fading shell.
As clearly then as this sweet night,
I'll still recall you kissed me well.

I risk no slip as I foretell
that, even though I be contrite
when I am dying, cell by cell
I'll still recall. You kissed me well.

The Chords
William O'Daly

*for Louis V. Johnson, in remembrance of Alex Johnson,
1988–2010*

And so we go, our hearts and minds aspire
in dew and in sunlight, open on song—
we come home to the vital moon,
our fingers picking and falling across
luminous strings, each discovered chord,
every rest and bridge the last. All of it,
the little things that confuse and steer us—
the asynchronous oaks, chromatic evergreens
swaying beside a high mountain road—
we lose our borders, the white sands
where we might dream returning the sound
to the original key, Adam's calm acceptance
of his fate, Eve's once perfect teeth. Beyond
the floating clouds, a silent hummingbird sails
on icy currents of grief. Soon everything is then
and gone, everything will be and is, and tomorrow lives
underground, with no aim but to inspire
the first breath. Every day the dogs
of defeat shall forgive us, and when night settles
we surrender to our life, sip the compassion
of our brothers and our sisters in a wineglass,
and keep the most bittersweet kiss
of our lover a little longer, before we are able
to cry again. We honor stone, the indelible storm,
the green tanager, prelude to our happiness.
The wind loves and leaves, inland souls
on a late bus discover the purpose of wings,
knowing the pure energy bequeathed by the young one
and the many who compose and sing,
who in memory invoke what they give.
We receive, give birth, strike a match

O'Daly, con't.

    to the hour, to the unknown
    as the rain begins to fall,
    as the bells awaken in our poem,
    in chords emerging, and we breathe.

The Apartment, Later

John Morgan

for 'Moo'

Like the click of a needle on an old LP—
those Sondheim hits you used to love,
"Though lately Broadway's lost its grip,"
you'd say—this living room, absent its rugs,
lamps, furniture and hanging plants;

and rising from the parquet floor, a scent
of camphor, pine, and some obscure
sixth sense of you. I cross the floor in socks,
recall six months ago, back from the
inadequate hospital: your wheelchair,

walker, oxygen, the home-care nurse,
our faulty hopes. This shadow on the wall
of Jeff's inherited Chagall. Down there's
the park at Washington Square we
strolled him to when he was small.

As panic seized your lungs, you screamed, "No,
no!" and never made it out of bed. With eyes
half shut, your final breath hovered as I held
my breath. The smell of death, particular and sweet,
the articulate flatness of your lips gone dumb.

They came by the back elevator
while Peter hurried up from NYU to see
his grandma newly dead. As tears streamed down
his cheeks and I sat numb, they shoved you in a sack
like meat and wheeled you out the door.

December Visit to Greenacres

Christine M. Kendall

On your grave a molehill piled high—
the soft wet mound disconcerting
as grass overgrowing your marker.

Crisp, dry leaves skitter across
the lawn helter-skelter
until a strong gust sweeps
them towards the gate.

I place the Christmas wreath
down—pegging it to the ground
so the Northeaster won't blow
it from here to who knows where.

Next time, next time—
I'll trim things up here,
sweep away the dirt filling
in the letters of your name.
Next time, next time—
I'll stay awhile longer.

Today, it's bitterly cold
and rain clouds head this
way, low and lumbering.
For now, for a moment,
just before I rise—

I remember you on your knees
beside me on the oval braided rug
when you would steal my nose
making me laugh until my sides hurt,
and that memory warms me.

Thus the World

Jennifer Bullis

*[T]hus the world is full of leaves and feathers,
and comfort, and instruction.*

—Mary Oliver, "The Dipper"

Over the grave of the old horse
gone one year, goldfinches—
dozens, hovering,

feasting on seeds of thistles
flourishing in the soil disturbed
by the backhoe.

Into the air the birds cast their trills,
their bright yellow, a little
comfort.

A Step Too Far

Paul Hunter

You cross the thawing valley
its icy ruts in plowed fields
till at the worst of it mired
knee-deep you break through
footsteps burdened stuck

in place where should you
lift a foot you lose a shoe
where you stagger until
there is no going on going
anywhere it's only stand or fall

where in this all but bottomless
bowl of gravy and goulash
overdone in the season just past
emptied out onto the plain
things sag down nothing drains

where in the sunset sinking
slowly you pause halfway
there back up and sidle onto
what you pray is still back there
a little firmer higher ground

Did You Ever Scream At A Pony?

Tony Curtis

I did, just the once, on the Errislanan Road—
That's way out west in Connemara—
I was coming back from Brendan's house
After a night on the whisky and beer.
I was all bendy like an accordion;
Floating along like a feather in the dark
Singing *The Rocky Road To Dublin*.
It was a night so black, so absolutely still,
I could have been in the grave.
Suddenly, a creature whinnied in my ear.
Every ghost and bog goblin that wandered the roads
Appeared before me in a moment of pure terror.
I screamed, and the darkness swallowed
Him up in a terrified drumming of hooves.

Beyond Her Lost Self

Paul Hunter

The sunken calf
found days too late
done in by lungworms
fallen deep in the leaves
of these woods overripe

dying halfgrown just enough
of a nuisance to others
the same age they'd walk off
not a thought left in her
sightless head not a cough

her empty body slumped
in this shaded pasture
of hollows and rich hills
an opportunity half-hidden
an invitation a reward

to the swarm drawn to her
brocade of ants and beetles
gaudy fringe of coon and opossum
her crows' officious inspection
her foxes' toothmark filagree

all round this faint near-collision
of rending and tearing this ballet
these passing chance to partake
to carry beyond her lost self
in bits her anonymous gift

The Handout
William O'Daly

The fear sneaks up on me—
the flickering streetlamp, the geraniums suddenly colorless
and isolated in their window box—
some measure of lightning is lost
at the rim of the darkening sky. I hear the hollow sound
of feet shuffle along the sidewalk—
they are our feet—then the empty horns
and the cautious hours begin, the uneasy absence
of young men who ride their dream horse
into the corral of a single thought,
and of women who ride the streetcar.
The thickening fog gathers, as it will,
accepts the figure huddled like a human
in the threadbare quilt. We are walking to our hotel,
where the carpet and the immortal art of sleep
will keep us. We pass a precise arc
of frozen shoulders, hooded head fallen
like a black petal in the corolla of night.
My pace quickens—my daughter, slowing
into her life, into the power of what she carries
in the fragrant bag swinging at her right hip,
stops and peers up. Barely suspecting what she knows,
I say "Let's go…" But she turns back
toward the blanketed life. He raises his head
a touch and looks at us, his eyes
catching the dim lights of docked ships.
She hands him half a cheeseburger and a heap of fries —
he gently accepts and in my shame
I learn how tonight he will eat, and later
in the cold and clanging air
the gulls will compete for a few missed crumbs
where we, at the same moment, say good night.

Barbara

J. Kaye Faulkner

The weather was miserable that night in 1984. I thought it was heavy rain for Seattle. I worked as a national representative for the American Federation of Teachers and I was on assignment. Since I was staying at the Camlin Hotel, I decided to have dinner in, rather than go out. I ate early, and alone, seldom company for any meal while working on the road. After dinner I walked across to the bar. Churchill has remarked, 'Americans quit drinking with dinner'. My friends and I never had any trouble continuing—except when we lacked the funds.

I sat at the bar drinking and reading when Barbara came in, unannounced. I was startled to have this tall and handsome blond woman sit next to me. I assumed that she was there to meet someone. She was certainly not there to meet me, and she offered no acknowledgment in my direction when I nodded at her.

She sat close, I supposed, because of the placement of the bar chairs. I was uncomfortable since she was stunning. I wasn't prepared for such a desirable looking woman in such a closed space. My mind wandered: She smelled as nice as she looked—and her presence demanded attention—she was not delicate (as I imagined Audrey Hepburn to be) that by touching her, she might break. I would have no problem touching her, with clear invitation—it was fear of consequences that would stop me.

She talked under her breath, and without apparent focus. I did not believe that she was drunk but rather angry—which is what turned out to be the case. I thought, *she is too young to be cynical,* but she sat there muttering. She had anger in her voice when she asked peremptorily: "What are you reading?" As if I were there to answer her questions.

My response could have been: it's none of your business—but she impressed me. I wanted to please. Besides, there is nothing like being paid a little attention, to get your attention—especially by someone as stunning as was this woman.

She turned a bit toward me and pushed me further. She wore a tight, silky dress. Its low cut showing nice cleavage with comfortably rounded breasts. The short jacket she wore settled back on her shoulders—watching her took my breath. "What are you reading that is so interesting?" I assumed she meant: "What are you reading that can possibly be more interesting than me."

Nothing, I thought. The prospects of passing the time with her as opposed to a good book left little room for doubt. I was reading *The Grand Panjandrum,* and I told her a little about the book. She picked up the theme and spun out some funny double meanings of words I mentioned. All the while anger punctuated her speech.

I thought, *what the hell.* "What is your problem?"

She said, "It is nothing. You could care less. You do not want to know."

Her response was good enough for me to inquire no further. I let it pass. However she continued on. She wanted to talk and I had no problem listening to her story. I offered to buy her a drink. She declined. It was to emerge why she declined. Though she ordered one and paid for it:

Barbara had just come from the bar at the Sheraton Hotel, where she had been with two men. One man she believed to be the boss of the younger, more handsome man. The men were engaged in finance. She had been picked up by the younger. The men bought several rounds of drinks and dinner may have been proffered, but not materialized. She had been invited to continue with them as they drank, when the conversation turned to a different and a meaner strain.

She said that the men knew she was a prostitute. (I did not know she was a prostitute. I was not even hoping she was a prostitute—though it did cross my mind. I should have realized that she was dressed for business.) The men teased her by denigrating what she did. They strung her along without consideration even after it was clear she had no alternatives because they had taken the leading edge of the evening. They had used up her time in the early evening without giving her money for it. She was angry that they had no more concern than to try to humiliate her. She would go without pay that evening. She needed work. She accused them of both being queer—and then stormed out of the Sheraton and walked to the Camlin.

We talked more about what she did and why she did it. She may have thought of me as a mark, when she first sat beside me—I didn't believe so. The Camlin is not so up-market as I imagined her prices, and not comparable to the Sheraton. (She was not concerned with marginal cost pricing at such a moment, either—I supposed.) In any event I talked too much and she had had a full evening of talkers. But she also wanted to talk; declining my offer of a drink was rather a clue as it should have been that I was not considered a prospective client.

I realized that this stunning woman while sharing her trials, her story had familiar themes, and almost accompanying sounds like a music score playing along with the drama of her circumstance. She said she had two small sons. She worked in a counseling center in Seattle. Whether it was the municipal operation with private funding from mixed sources, I could not discern. As a national union representative I assumed she had low wages, no union and no recourse in the workplace. She supplemented her income by hooking to take care of herself and her boys.

I have spent much of my life listening to similar stories. All of us have problems, frequently caused by someone in authority or the consequences of social relations. This was a variation on the theme by explicitly turning to what we call prostitution. (Many people do turn to alternatives going by different names: the process is comparable.) I come to these conversations without complaint. The issues are sometimes impossible to resolve—since the parties are so committed to their own positions, standings or strategies. (I have, from time to time, quoted an insight by Gladstone: "Most men would rather that you heard their story than granted their demand".)

Barbara needed a union at the counseling center. I asked why she did not organize one? She was anti-union.

She said, "Unions have never helped."

I said, "You have to join—organize. Unions are not welfare organization going about doing good for any offhand employee."

She was angry with her employer, fellow workers, her clientele and her failure to provide for her kids. "We are not paid enough."

It was a heavy moment filled with this powerful woman. She was sexually awesome and desirable. Her beauty and intelligence brought together in an organized effort, I supposed, could have achieved results in her full-time job action. I liked her strength and with her anger focused—I felt she could be successful in forming a union.

I objected to the way she personalized her ills—since it locked her into continuing what she was doing. Her anger would not in the least lead to emancipatory ends unless better focused.

The unions, she repeated, would not help; unions were all bullshit.

I responded with, "Build your own union and affiliate with whom you please. Unions are not bullshit but you have to work to achieve what you say you want."

Parenthetically I did not believe for a moment her complaint that she hooked to increase only the family income—there were alternatives. Like most people with excuses for what they are doing they are getting other things out of the part-time effort whatever it might be—the overtime work at a factory or as in this case, hooking.

She had a good deal in common with college professors with whom I had dealt with for years. They want better things, but they want someone else to do it for them—something for nothing anoint us with the magic to secure additional income without the understanding that workers must unite politically to achieve the results to better their lives.

If you need it fixed: organize! You cannot blame someone else for what you have permitted to happen to you—especially when it is your own inaction. Your mother is not here to fix it for you.

Barbara and I talked for the rest of the evening. I understood the mix of criticism and failure. I also know how I would have approached a solution, but like so many others who crossed my path she would rather slog on, and that night I was there to listen and only suggest.

We had become something close to friends through the evening of conversation and an advisory code of conduct emerged. Something called professionalism seemingly characterized our last hour or so of conversation by which is meant objective advice. She gave me her telephone number with only her first name listed. I did not call her since there was little point unless she was willing to organize—it was unlikely and I needed to be assigned before I got myself into her mess.

I bid her goodnight. I headed to my room alone. I did not want nor did I need any help getting to bed. I was the organizer and she my client—whatever profession she followed whether it was social worker or prostitute. She got a good deal of good advice from me, with no strings attached and would be better off if she were to act on that advice.

The failure to recognize our alienated relationships is sometimes astounding. We are all prostitutes to some degree. How many of us are emancipated well enough to stand alone? We need the employment commitment, direction and forthcoming payments from an employer to survive.

The criticism of a woman who is reduced to selling her body is little different than the worker who sells himself to the auto company manufacturer for an income in which he has little or no choice. It is the moral overlay that elicits the condemnation.

It is difficult for us to survive in the circumstances of capitalism and the false consciousness of competition is just one of the many illusions we live with. There is also the prospect of an organized society that is far better than what we now have.

Blame (a partial list)

Larry Crist

First, i blame this awkward opening for which i have only myself to blame.
I blame protocol which says everything must have a beginning.
I blame you for just sitting there and beat my chest, because it's the only acceptable
portion of my body i can beat in public, but it's early;
ask not for whom the blame tolls, all will unfold...
Blame isms and Greeks, Sisyphus and rock, Aristotle and his poetics
Rabelais' rants, Cervantes, Shakespeare and everything anyone has ever written.
Blame Guttenburg, Simon and Schuster, Grove Press, those who don't read and those
who read too much into everything.
Blame beans, magical, gaseous and metaphorical; those who crunch fantastical.
Blame nations & Haitians, Cortez, Columbus & Custer, blame the French, Dutch,
British. Blame the president, who carries the same blame as stained the one before;
Blame power and power outages. Blame hip-hop, rap, soul, country, blame the FCC &
long playing LPs. Blame tv, blame You Tube and fast food; blame the waitress, blame
that thing she forgot that took too long.
Blame traffic and weather, whether or not it be fair... Blame god, blame that which
cannot blame back. Blame mom, blame dad, blame their divorce, blame 'em just cause.
Blame their youth, their era, blame society and the society it keeps.
Write a poem; blame that; blame your writing teacher. Blame everyone who failed to
stop you. Blame boredom and whoredom and sub standard of living standardly.
Blame the church, blame catholics, jews, christians, mormons, muslims, hindus,
zoroastrians, confucians and your little buddha too.
Blame continental drift, whoever was at fault, those continents should pay more
attention.
Blame cell phones and texting. Blame teenagers. Blame technology. Blame city council,

Crist, con't.

city management, underground overcosts, blame the bridge for being up and that boat that sailed belowly too slowly.
Blame the homeless. Blame and kick everything especially those without legs.
Blame congress and cronies, back scratchers, palm greasers, midnight wheeler-dealers, ankle-grabbers, procrastinators & eager fellatiators, legislators, floggers & bloggers, self starters, latecomers and those who show-up on time with their own excuses.
Blame emotions, hormones, high fructose corn syrup. Blame men & women and trannys in transition. Blame lubricants, flies in ointment, bees in bonnets, embedded saddle burrs, open toed sandals, engine grit, wayward pebbles, blisters, splinters, static cling, errant ball bearings, lost marbles, waxy build-up, ripped nails, dull razors, cold sores, artificial artifacts, esoteric heirlooms, frisky fornicators, hyperactivity and ghosts in the machine.
Blame that smug mechanic at Jiffy Lube who said everything looked okay.
Blame liberals, and all windbag demigods, radio ranters, easy listening listeners, Muzac, NPR pledge drives and supporting members like you & me.

I blame the first joint i ever smoked and that final drink i had night before last.
I blame Alan Smoot who lived across the street and who i used to fight every saturday afternoon because there was nothing else to do.
There's lots of blame to go around. I'd like to blame everything i have so far failed to blame because blame seemed too easy and obvious, a cop-out, too damn blameworthy, like lawyers for instance or the poems of John Donne, people who wear thick coats on hot days without sweating, vegetarians, vulgarians, tobacco chewers, fishing lures.

Special shout out blame to the sun, moon, stars, and whomever said Pluto could no longer be a planet. I blame spirituality, central heating, indoor plumbing, penicillin, badly drawn cartoons, Republicans and Ralph Nader. I blame every film ever made by John Wayne and John Ford and those they made together i blame doubly. I blame Hope & Crosby, Clinton's second term, rising oil prices and falling standardized test scores. I

Crist, con't.

blame fluoride, lead in the pipes, in the paint, lead in the goalie's ass which led to yet another tie, with four star blame to the academy for which it stands, scapegoats in the rough, genetics in general, fireworks and the tall dry grass, hot-pants, fish-nets, dominatrixes, and a general disregard for the importance of coasters in our society. I blame popsicles, pesticides, regicide, patricide, genocide on ferons, freons, pheromones and a lack of leadership among our stolen elected officials, as well as the lyrics of Johnny Mercer and all music featuring the accordion or bagpipes. Most of all i blame the system for which it stands especially the Masons and other not-so-secret societies, whose names escape me, who knew, or should have known, and should accept the lionshare of blame, with lone exception to the pride-less lion itself, hunted and harried, looking up from an eviscerated lamb with blood on its mane, its face & paws, corralled by corporate wolves, while introducing yet another lame-ass movie we've already seen, roaring twice and pleading forgiveness for having been born a beast.

Author Notes

Gailmarie Pahmeier has been a Nevadan for nearly 30 years. She currently teaches creative writing and contemporary literature courses at the University of Nevada, where she has been honored with the Alan Bible Teaching Excellence Award and the University Distinguished Teacher Award. She is also on the faculty of the low residency MFA Program at Sierra Nevada College. A frequent Pushcart Prize nominee, her work has garnered a number of awards, including a Witter Bynner Poetry Fellowship and two Artist Fellowships from the Nevada Arts Council and has been widely published in literary journals and anthologies. She is the author of *The House on Breakaheart Road* and also the author of three chapbooks, the most recent of which, *Shake It and It Snows,* won the 2009 Coal Hill Chapbook Award from Autumn House Press. In 2007, she received the Governor's Award for Excellence in the Arts from the State of Nevada. Pgs. 5-7, 146-147, 171-172.

Mary's Bio of Dave:

David Lee is the author of numerous poetry collections, including *The Porcine Legacy* (1974), *Driving and Drinking* (1979), *The Porcine Canticles* (1984), *Wayburne Pig* (1997), *News from Down to the Café: New Poems* (1999), and *A Legacy of Shadows: Selected Poems* (1999). Born in West Texas, Lee has been a boxer, pig farmer, seminary student, cotton mill worker, and the only white baseball player for a Negro League team. He received a PhD in literature, with a concentration in the poetry of John Milton, from the University of Utah. He retired as Chairman of the Humanities Department at Southern Utah University. The first poet laureate of Utah, Lee received the Utah Governor's Award for lifetime achievement in the arts. His evocative *So Quietly the Earth* (2004) was named to "Best Books of the

David Lee, con't.

Year" list by the New York Public Library. *Stone Wind Water* is a sequel to that work.

Dave's Bio of Dave:

David Lee, quasi-impervious wanderer, splits his time between Bandera, Texas; Seaside, Oregon; and the Cascade River, Washington, where he scribbles and wanders available trails and byways, all at about the same rate and pace. He is in intense training to achieve his goal of becoming a World Class Piddler. Pgs. 8-11.

Michael Daley is the author of three collections of poetry. His most recent, *Moonlight in the Redemptive Forest* (Pleasure Boat Studio, 2010) includes a CD. His translation of Lucia Gazzino's *Alter Mundus* is forthcoming from World Enough Writers. Pgs. 12, 89.

Sally Green is a poet, printer, book designer, calligrapher—and co-publisher of the award-winning Brooding Heron Press, which publishes fine, letterpressed editions of poetry (Gary Snyder, Denise Levertov, Donald Hall, Hayden Carruth, John Haines, etc.). In 2008, Pacific Lutheran University awarded her a Stanley W. Lindberg Editor's Award for excellence. Her own poems have appeared in *The Poets Guide to the Birds* (Anhinga Press), *The Ladies Printing Bee*, *The Planet Earth Poetry Anthology* (Leaf Press), two limited edition chapbooks, *Instead of Sleeping* and *Full Immersion*, as well as other publications. She was a featured poet at the annual Lower Columbia College Literary Festival, the Planet Earth Poetry Reading series at The Moka House in Victoria, B.C., and the Northwind Reading Series in Port Townsend, WA. Pgs. 13, 165-167.

Bryce Milligan has lived in San Antonio, Texas since 1977. Among other things, he has been a folksinger, a maker of guitars, drums and dulcimers, a carpenter, a rare book bibliographer and appraiser, a college English and creative

Milligan, con't.

writing instructor, a poet-in-the-schools, an arts administrator, a book and magazine editor, a book designer, and a publisher. As a writer, he has been a newspaper columnist, a freelance journalist, a scholar, a novelist, a poet, a playwright, and an essayist. Milligan is the publisher of Wings Press and the author of four collections of poetry, *Daysleepers & Other Poems* (1984), *Litany Sung at Hell's Gate* (1991), *From Inside the Tree* (cassette, 1990 and 1994), *Working the Stone* (Wings Press, 1994), *Alms for Oblivion: A Poem in Seven Parts* (London: Aark Arts, 2003) and *Lost and Certain of It* (London: Aark Arts, 2006). Pgs. 14-15.

Jim Milstead retired after many years of rearing cockroaches, houseflies, California oakworms, cabbage whites, wax moths, silkworms, and bark beetles. Now he writes about jellyfish, tuna, ants, antlions, flatworms, amoebae, bark beetles, cockroaches, groundhogs, and whales. He vents his overloaded spleen on Facebook. IWS member. Pgs. 16-18.

Larry Crist lives in Seattle. He is originally from California, specifically Humboldt County (Bay Area & elsewhere). He has also lived in Chicago, London, Houston and Philadelphia where he attended Temple University earning an MFA in theatre. Larry's been widely published. Some of his favorites are *Pearl, Rattle, Slipstream, Evening Street Review, Dos Passos Review, Floating Bridge Press, Alimentum* and many others. Larry has three Pushcart nominations and is particularly pleased to find himself inside the covers of *Clover* now for the third time. Pgs. 19-26, 219-221.

Jon D. Lee published his first book of poetry—*Ode to Brian: The Long Season*—in 2006. He received his PhD in folklore from Memorial University of Newfoundland in 2009 and currently lives in Boston, where he teaches literature at various universities and is hard at work on a second book of poetry as well as a collection of short stories. Pgs. 27, 51, 124-140, 201.

Andrea Carter is nearing the finish line of her first novel, *A Mouthful of Murder*. She works as a technical writer and teacher in Bellingham and is a rabid Seattle Sounders fan. IWS member. Pgs. 28, 79-80, 141.

Elizabeth Thrall is a senior at Olivet Nazarene University near Chicago. She is majoring in English education and history. She immensely enjoys reading, writing, and cooking. "Fairy Tale" is her first published poem. Pg. 29.

Seren Fargo, once a wildlife researcher with the U.S. Forest Service, now writes poetry, particularly Japanese-form poetry, which she finds satisfies both her creative side and her scientific side. In 2009, she founded the Bellingham Haiku Group, which she currently coordinates. Her work has won several awards and has been published in many journals in the United States and internationally. She lives with her three cats, Badger, Princess Kita, and 20-year-old Neptune. Pgs. 30, 59.

Norman L. Green now lives in Bellingham. He is a recovering playwright from Canada, by way of Arkansas and Texas and has been unable to tell his own lies from his truths for more than 50 years. He posts his dreams at NormanLGreen.wordpress.com and visits various point in the Twentieth Century in his fiction. IWS member. Pgs. 31-35.

Shelley Muzzy lives in Bellingham and is a member of the Independent Writers' Studio. She is currently working on her first novel and regularly writes a radio comedy script for the Chuckanut Radio Hour. Her work has been published in the first three editions of *Clover* and she contributes to an online dance magazine. Pgs. 36-43.

Rosemerry Wahtola Trommer lives in Southwest Colorado. Favorite four-word mantra: *I am still learning.* Favorite one-word mantra: *Adjust.* A new collection, *The Less I Hold,* was released in November, 2012 from Turkey Buzzard Press. Pgs. 44-45, 105-106.

Laurel Rust's first collection of poetry, *What Is Given* was published by Brooding Heron Press. Her poems have appeared in many magazines. She earned a degree from the University of Washington and lives off the coast of northwest Washington on Orcas Island, where she works full time at the Orcas ferry terminal. Pgs. 46, 70, 111.

Dayna Patterson recently moved to the Northwest from Texas. She is the mother of two and poetry editor for *Psaltery & Lyre*. Her chapbooks, *Loose Threads* and *Mothering*, are available from Flutter Press. Her creative works have appeared or are forthcoming in *Persona, WordsWork, Exponent II, Flutter Poetry Journal, Segullah, FMH, Borderline*, and many others. Pgs. 47-48, 90.

Tony Curtis was born in Dublin, Ireland. He is the author of eight collections of poetry, the most recent being *Folk* (Arc Publications, 2011) and with the photographer Liam Blake *Sand Works: a book of Photographs and Haiku* (Real Ireland, 2011). Tony is currently working on a book of poems and photographs about that most beautiful of creatures, the Connemara Pony. He is a member of Aosdána, the Irish Academy of Arts. Pgs. 49, 61, 209.

Andrew Shattuck McBride is a Bellingham-based writer and editor. He has a short story published in *Whatcom WRITES!*, and poems published or forthcoming in *Platte Valley Review, Caesura*, and *Magnapoets*, among others. His poem "Grace" won a merit award in the 2012 Sue C. Boynton Poetry Contest. His current projects include a linked short story collection. www.andrewsmcbride.wordpress.com. Pgs. 50, 78, 169.

Janet Bergstrom retired from teaching in 2006. She now works in her gardens, makes art, writes stories, and travels with her husband. Her work has been published online in *More Magazine* and she received an honorable mention in the *Writer's Digest* Writers Competition. She is working on

Bergstrom, con't.

a collection of travel stories entitled *Travel Adventures of Ordinary People*. Her memoir, *Ta Bu or Not Ta Bu: True Tales of an Aging Hippie Chick* is available at Amazon or from her blog at http://tabuuornottabuu.wordpress.com. IWS member. Pgs. 52-58.

Nancy Takacs lives in Price, Utah, and teaches an ongoing nature poetry workshop at the Senior Citizen Center there. A former wilderness studies and creative writing instructor at the College of Eastern Utah, her latest book is *Juniper* from Limberlost Press. Pgs. 60, 91-92, 103-104.

Alan Cohen lives in the land of bark and leaves in southeast Ohio. He is a retired teacher, avid naturalist, adventure traveler and student of the natural world. He is the founder and facilitator of Power of Poetry, a festival that for 11 years has been healing the misdeads perpetrated by evil 7th grade teachers on the poetic minds of their students by showing that poetry is inspiring, rich, beauty-full, and even fun. Alan compiled *Red Thread Gold Thread*, an anthology of essays and poems from more than fifty poets from around the country. A sequel is in the works. More information at www.powerofpoetry.org, and at www.redthreadgoldthread.com. Pg. 62.

Samuel Green was born in Sedro-Woolley, Washington, and raised in the nearby fishing and mill town of Anacortes. After four years in the military, including service in Antarctica and South Vietnam, he attended college under the Veterans Vocational Rehabilitation Program, earning degrees from Highline Community College and Western Washington University (BA & MA). A 36-year veteran as a poet-in-the-schools, he has taught in hundreds of classrooms around Washington State. He has also been a visiting professor at Southern Utah University, Western Wyoming Community College, Colorado College, and served nine winter terms as Distinguished Visiting Northwest

Samuel Green, con't.

Writer at Seattle University. Poems have appeared in *Poetry, Poetry Northwest, Poet & Critic, Poetry East, Southern Poetry Review, Prairie Schooner,* and *Puerto del Sol* among others. Among his ten collections of poems are *Vertebrae: Poems 1972-1994* (Eastern Washington University Press) and *The Grace of Necessity* (Carnegie-Mellon University Press), which won the 2008 Washington State Book Award for Poetry. Poems in this volume of *Clover* will be found in *The Fierce Bird of Memory*, due out in 2014 from Carnegie Mellon University Press. He has lived for 30 years off the grid on remote Waldron Island off the Washington coast in a log house he built himself after living in a tent for three years. He is, with his wife, Sally, co-editor of the award-winning Brooding Heron Press, which produces fine, letterpressed volumes (Donald Hall, James Laughlin, Denise Levertov, Gary Snyder, Pattiann Rogers, Jane Hirshfield, Hayden Carruth, among many). In December, 2007, he was named as the inaugural poet laureate for the State of Washington. A memoir, *First Up: Barnstorming for Poetry*, about his two years as laureate, recently appeared from Chuckanut Editions, Village Books, in Bellingham. Other honors include a National Endowment for the Arts Fellowship in Poetry and an Artist Trust Fellowship in Literature. He served on the NEA's Fellowship panel for the 2010 fellowships. Pgs. 63, 87, 112, 154-155, 200.

William O'Daly is a poet, translator, and fiction writer. His translations include eight books of the poetry of Chilean Nobel laureate Pablo Neruda, all published with Copper Canyon Press. Also from Copper Canyon, he published a chapbook of his own poems, *The Whale in the Web*. He was a finalist for the 2006 Quill Award in Poetry and was profiled on NBC's The Today Show. A National Endowment for the Arts Fellow, his poems, translations, essays, and reviews have appeared widely in magazines and anthologies. With co-author Han-ping Chin, William recently completed a historical novel, *This Earthly Life,* which was awarded as a

O'Daly, con't.

finalist in Narrative's 2009 Fall Story Contest. He also has received national and regional honors for literary editing and instructional design. Pgs. 64-65, 203-204, 211.

Mikel Vause holds a PhD from Bowling Green University and is a professor of English at Weber State University where he serves as director of Environmental Studies. He is author of numerous articles, poems, and short stories that have appeared in various books, magazines and journals and is thrilled to have his poems appear in *Clover, A Literary Rag*. He is also author of four collections of poems: *I Knew It Would Come to This*; *At the Edge of Things*; *Looking for the Old Crown* (a poetic guidebook to interesting and out-of-the-way places in Great Britain); and *The Scent of Juniper: Poems of the Himalayas*. Pgs. 66-67, 68, 107-108.

Peggy Shumaker served as Alaska State Writer Laureate for 2010-2012. *Toucan Nest*, her new book of poems, grew from an eco-arts workshop in Costa Rica. The book will be published in 2013 by Red Hen Press. Shumaker is founding editor of Boreal Books, publisher of literature and fine art from Alaska, and she edits the Alaska Literary Series at University of Alaska Press. Visit her website at peggyshumaker.com. Pgs. 109, 160.

Paulann Petersen is Oregon's sixth poet laureate. She has five full-length books of poetry: *The Wild Awake, Blood-Silk, A Bride of Narrow Escape, Kindle,* and *The Voluptuary*. Her most recent publication is *Shimmer and Drone*, a chapbook of poems about India. She was a Stegner Fellow at Stanford University, and the recipient of the 2006 Holbrook Award from the Oregon Literary Arts. She serves on the board of Friends of William Stafford, organizing the January Stafford Birthday Events. Pgs. 71-72, 102.

Susan J. Erickson's poems appear recently in *Crab Creek Review, Raven Chronicles, Switched-on-Gutenberg, Knockout*

Erickson, con't.

Literary Review, Floating Bridge Review and *The Lyric.* She lives in Bellingham, Washington where she helped establish the Sue C. Boynton Poetry Walk. She is working on a manuscript of poems in women's voices. Pg. 73.

Denise duMaurier lives in Bellingham, Washington. She has also lived in Pittsburgh, New York City, London, and Minneapolis. Studied creative writing for ten years at The Loft Literary Center in Minneapolis and graduated from the Foreword/Master Track program there. She has two poetry books in print: *Abandoning the Raft* and *Follow Me Down.* Pg. 74.

Christine M. Kendall left Whatcom County to head over the mountains to her new home on 20 acres in Twisp, Washington. One of her saddest farewells, she said was to IWS and the Wednesday evening group who along with Mary generously gave suggestions for her work, shared their writing and musings along with lots of chocolate and laughter. She intends to plan trips to Bellingham to coincide with Wednesday evenings hoping there will always be a chair that's vacant at the writers' studio. Besides her poetry appearing in *Clover* she was recently published by *Windfall Press.* IWS member. Pgs. 75, 115, 152, 206.

Shannon Laws lives in Bellingham, Washington. Her blog Madrona Grove is a sharing of encounters and personal insights. Shannon is active in the local writer community attending monthly open mics and hosts Village Book's Poetry Group. She is also a board member of Teaching and Learning Arts (TALA), a local group of artists that promotes the teaching of science and art. Shannon is a volunteer radio host at Bellingham's SPARK Museum community station KMRE 102.3. http://splawssji.blogspot.com. Pgs. 76-77.

Jim Reese is an associate professor of English, director of the Great Plains Writers' Tour at Mount Marty College

Reese, con't.

in Yankton, South Dakota, and editor-in-chief of *Paddle-Fish*. Reese's poetry and prose have been widely published, most recently in *New York Quarterly, Poetry East, Paterson Literary Review, Louisiana Literature Review, Connecticut Review*, and elsewhere. His new book *ghost on 3rd* (NYQ Books, 2010) was a finalist for the 2010 Milt Kessler Poetry Award. Since 2008, Jim has been one of five artists-in-residence throughout the country who are part of the National Endowment for the Art's interagency initiative with the Department of Justice's Federal Bureau of Prisons. Jim and his family live in southern South Dakota, near John Wesley Powell's one hundredth meridian—better than most determinants for where the American West begins. Pgs. 81-82, 143.

Janet Oakley is a writer, historian, and a practicing gardener. Her personal essays appear in the Cup Of Comfort series. *Tree Soldier*, a novel of the Great Depression won a 2012 Epic ebook award for historical fiction as well as a 2012 grand prize from *Chanticleer Book Reviews*. Recently, Humanities Washington selected her as a 2012-2014 speaker. Her articles on Washington State history are at Historylink.org and in December her article on the ship, *Ann Parry* will be the lead article in the prestigious journal, *Sea Chest*. She is known to churn butter with 3rd and 5th graders and likes a good historical tale. She writes every day no matter what. Pgs. 83-84.

James Bertolino's twenty-seventh collection of poetry, *Every Wound Has a Rhythm*, was published in 2012 by World Enough Writers. He's received a number of national awards and has taught poetry writing at Cornell University, University of Cincinnati, Willamette University, and Western Washington University. Now retired, he lives outside Bellingham, with his new wife, Anita Boyle. Pgs. 85, 114, 142.

Joseph Powell teaches at Central Washington University. He has published four books of poetry, the most recent is *Hard Earth* (March Street Press, 2010). A new collection, *Preamble to the Afterlife*, is seeking its home in print. Pgs. 86, 110.

Judith Azrael was born in Baltimore, Maryland. A graduate of the University of Wisconsin, she holds an MFA from the University of Oregon. She has taught writing workshops at art centers and colleges and has been a visiting writer at Western Washington University. She has published four books of poetry: *Fire in August* (Zeitgeist Press); *Fields of Light* (Cassiopeia Press); *Antelope are Running;* and, *Apple Tree Poems* (both from Confluence Press). Her works have appeared in anthologies and numerous magazines, including *Harvard Review, The Minnesota Review*, and others. Her book, *Wherever I Wander* (Impassio Press), was published in 2004. She travels to Greece whenever she can and is now working on a full-length book set in the Greek islands. Pgs. 88, 153, 161.

J. Jamieson Woods is originally from the great land to the north and still slips an occasional "eh" into conversation. She has been writing for many years but since joining the IWS she has taken her writing to a more committed level. She spends a great deal of time teaching little children and enjoys it immensely. Pgs. 93-101.

Sara E. Simard's poems portray a spirited and gentle woman. Sara lives with her husband Steve in Bellingham. Her first book of poetry, *Water Poems* was published in 2007. IWS member. Pgs. 113.

Rosalyn Ostler, Cottonwood Heights, Utah, was born in Phoenix, spent a great tomboy childhood in a tiny Missouri town. She met her husband Robert during grass fights, Kick-the-Can, and free-for-all basketball in Nephi, Utah.

Ostler, con't.

For over 60 years, Rose and Bob have lived in the Salt Lake valley. She is wife, mother of 7, grandmother, and great-grandmother. She served as president of Utah State Poetry Society and is now an officer; she has many years of service as a Boy Scout leader and church teacher. She loves kids and teens—and poets! She is a co-author of *By the Throat*, which took 2nd place in a Writers' Digest competition for self-published poetry books. Her book, *Walking the Earth Barefoot*, won publication, making her UTSPS 2010 Poet of the Year. Pgs. 116-117, 163-164, 202.

Betty Scott's writings have appeared in *Bellowing Arc, Bellingham Review, Borders, fathoms, The Kumquat Challenge, Jeopardy* and others. She wrote a bi-monthly column for the Wentachee World for five years. In May of 2012, she received the Empowered Poet for Peace Award by the World Poetry International of Richmond, Canada, and was featured on their website in August of that year. In 2010, she won a poetry award at Surrey International Writer's Conference. She co-judged the Bellingham's Sue Boynton Poetry Contest in 2012, and was a featured writer, and workshop presenter at the Chuckanut Writers Conference in Bellingham. Pg. 118.

Allen Frost is the author of *The Mermaid Translation* (Bird Dog Publishing, 2010). He is the editor of *Selected Correspondence of Kenneth Patchett* (Bottom Dog Press, 2012). His short story collection is forthcoming. http://allenfrost-library.blogspot.com. Pgs. 119-120.

John Morgan has published four books of poetry, most recently *Spear-Fishing On The Chatanika: New And Selected Poems* (Salmon Poetry). A collection of his essays, *Forms Of Feeling: Poetry In Our Lives*, was published in 2012. His work has appeared in *The New Yorker, Poetry, American Poetry Review, The New Republic, The Paris Review*, and many other magazines. In 2009, he served as the first writer-in-residence at Denali National Park. Pgs. 121, 156-157, 205.

Luther Allen grew up in the Southwest and moved to Washington about 20 years ago. He facilitates SpeakEasy, a community poetry reading series. He published a 365 poem manuscript in 2010 about nature/insight/perception entitled *The View from Lummi Island.* Pg. 122.

Stephanie Cosky Hopkinson is learning to live in the moment. In this moment, maple trees are more limb than leaf and Maggie the dog lies with her belly towards the heater vent and her eyes on the birds outside. In a past moment, her poem "The day her life changed" was danced at Bellingham's 2012 *Phrasings.* IWS member. Pgs. 123, 198-199.

Nancy Canyon's writing is published in *Labyrinth, Able Muse, Water~Stone Review, Fourth Genre, Main Street Rag, Floating Bridge Review,* and more. She is a fiction editor for *Crab Creek Review*, writing instructor for Whatcom Community College and Western's Academy of Life Long Learning, a visual artist, and massage therapist in private practice. She holds an MFA in creative writing from Pacific Lutheran University and is currently revising her third novel. Her ebook of short-shorts can be seen at http://tinyurl.com/6mu5k74. Pgs. 144, 162.

Simon Perchik is an attorney whose poems have appeared in *Partisan Review, The Nation, The New Yorker,* and elsewhere. For more information, including free ebooks, his essay titled "Magic, Illusion and Other Realities," and a complete bibliography, visit his website at www.simonperchik.com. Pg. 145.

Mary Elizabeth Gillilan's gratitude extends outward. It catches hold on *Clover, A Literary Rag,* and shines. Her children sustain the joy factor and her dogs and cat add variety. Poetry saved her. http://independentwritersstudio.com. Pgs. 69, 148-149.

Anita K. Boyle is a poet, artist, and freelance graphic designer. She is the author of *What the Alder Told Me* (MoonPathPress, 2011), and *Bamboo Equals Loon* (Egress Studio Press, 2001). She lives with her husband, James Bertolino, near an influential pond outside Bellingham. Pgs. 150-151.

Richard Lee Harris moved with his parents and sister to the south side of the Skagit River at Rockport, Washington, in 1937. Harris has been a Bellingham writer for more than 20 years. He published *Reimagine: Poems, 1993-2009* in 2010 and will publish *Distant Times, Distant Places* later this year. He is also joining poetry and prose into a memoir about growing up in the Upper Skagit River Valley. You may learn more about Dick's poems and writing at http://blog.richardleeharris.net. Pgs. 158-159.

Randy Phillis' work has appeared in a wide range of journals, including *Iowa Review, Denver Quarterly, Florida Review* and *South Carolina Review*. He has published two books with small presses. He teaches writing and American literature at Colorado Mesa University, where he edits *Pinyon*. Pg. 168.

C.M. Clarke is originally from Wisconsin and now lives in Seattle, where she divides her time between poetry and biology. She was most recently published in *DMQ Review* and her poetry has received awards from the Seattle Public Library and the Redmond Arts Council. She is a member of the Washington Poets Association and can be found listening to or reading poetry at venues throughout the Greater Seattle area. Pg. 170.

Neil Harrison teaches English and creative writing at Northeast Community College in Norfolk, Nebraska where he coordinates the Visiting Writers Series. His previous publications include a chapbook, *Story* (Logan House Press, 1995 and 1996), and the collections *In a River of Wind*

Harrison, con't.

(Bridge Burner's Publishing, 2000), *Into the River Canyon at Dusk* (Lone Willow Press, 2005), and *Back in the Animal Kingdom* (Pinyon Publishing, 2011). Pg. 173.

Bruce Douglas Reeve's novella, *Delphine*, won the Clay Reynolds Novella Competition (Texas Review Press, 2012). His novels include: *The Night Action* (New American Library and Signet Books); *Man on Fire* (Pyramid Books); and, *Street Smarts* (Beaufort Books and Ace Books.) His short fiction has appeared in *The High Plains Literary Review, Runner's World Annual, Hawaii Review*, and many others. Some of his short stories,are available at www.anthologybuilder.com. For more information visit his blog: http://redroom.com/member/bruce-douglas-reeves/blog. Pgs. 174-197.

Jennifer Bullis, originally from Reno, Nevada, has lived in Bellingham for 17 years. Her poems appear in *Iron Horse Literary Review, Natural Bridge, Conversations Across Borders, Floating Bridge Review,* and *Umbrella*. She has won The Pitch contest at *Poetry Northwest* and received Honorable Mention in the Tupelo Press Poetry Project. Her chapbook, *Impossible Lessons*, is forthcoming from MoonPath Press in spring 2013. Pg. 207.

Paul Hunter lives in Seattle, where he has worked as a teacher, and for the past 18 years has published letterpress books and broadsides under the imprint of Wood Works. His farming poems have been reviewed in the New York Times and have received the Washington State Book Award. He has been a featured poet on PBS' The NewsHour. His new book, *Stubble Field*, is a fourth collection of farming poems from Silverfish Review Press. Pgs. 208, 210.

J. Kaye Faulkner published his memoirs, *The Road From Moab*, in July of 2011. The essays reflect his time as a university professor at Western Washington University and as a union organizer for university professors. Born in Thomp-

Faulkner, con't.

son Springs, Utah, in 1932, Faulkner's blue collar work ethic made his ascension from TV repairman to scholar possible. He lives in Bellingham with his lovely wife, Mollie. Started writing with Mary Gillilan's groups in 1993. IWS member. Pgs. 212-218.